Matthias Kistl

How can the euro area crisis be solved in the long run?

Bibliografische Information der Deutschen Nationalbibliothek:

Die Deutsche Nationalbibliothek verzeichnet diese Publikation in der Deutschen Nationalbibliografie; detaillierte bibliografische Daten sind im Internet über http://dnb.d-nb.de abrufbar.

Impressum:

Ein Imprint der Open Publishing GmbH

Druck und Bindung: Books on Demand GmbH, Norderstedt, Germany

Covergestaltung: Open Publishing GmbH

Table of Contents

Abbreviations 5

Table of graphs 8

1 Introduction 9

2 Origins of the euro area crisis 12

2.1 Theory: Optimum currency areas 12

2.2 Design flaws in the EMU 16

3 Rescue operations and structural reforms: what was done to prevent the break-up of the eurozone? 46

3.1 Macroeconomic (rescue) measures 46

3.2 Monetary Policy 50

3.3 Banking Union 55

4 Assessment and problems still to be solved 57

4.1 Macroeconomic measures 57

4.2 Monetary Policy 65

4.3 Banking Union 68

4.4 Competitiveness levels 70

4.5 Further obstacles and problems 75

4.6 Interim Conclusion 77

5 Proposals 79

5.1 Proposals including more integration in the eurozone 80

5.2 Proposals including more individual responsibility and/or less integration in the eurozone 107

6 Assessment **117**

7 Conclusion **124**

Bibliography **127**

List of Abbreviations

ABS	Asset-Backed Securities
ABSPP	Asset-Backed Securities Purchase Program
APP	Asset Purchase Program
BRRD	Bank Recovery and Resolution Directive
CBPP3	Covered Bond Purchase Program 3
CompNet	Competitiveness Research Network
CPI	Consumer Price Index
CRD IV	Capital Requirements Directive IV
CSPP	Corporate Sector Purchase Program
DGS	Deposit Guarantee Scheme
DGSD	Deposit Guarantee Scheme Directive
DMO	Debt Management Office
EAPP	Expanded Asset Purchase Program
EBA	European Banking Authority
ECB	European Central Bank
ECOFIN	Economic and Financial Affairs Council
EDA	European Debt Agency
EDIS	European Deposit Insurance Scheme
EFSF	European Financial Stability Facility
EFSM	European Financial Stability Mechanism
EIP	Excessive Imbalance Procedure
EIPS	European Investment Protection Scheme
EJBies	European Junior Bonds
ELA	Emergency Liquidity Assistance
EMF	European Monetary Fund
EMU	European Monetary Union
ERF	European Redemption Fund

ERM II	European Exchange Rate Mechanism II
ERP	European Redemption Pact
ESBies	European Safe Bonds
ESM	European Stability Mechanism
ESRB	European Systemic Risk Board
EU	European Union
EUBS	European Unemployment Benefit Scheme
G7	Group of Seven
GCEE	German Council of Economic Experts
GDP	Gross Domestic Product
GIPSIC	Greece, Ireland, Portugal, Spain, Italy, Cyprus
HCI	Harmonized Competitiveness Indicator
IMF	International Monetary Fund
LOLR	Lender of Last Resort
MFI	Monetary Financial Institution
MIP	Macroeconomic Imbalance Procedure
OCA	Optimum Currency Area
OMT	Outright Monetary Transactions
PSPP	Public Sector Purchase Program
REER	Real Effective Exchange Rate
SGP	Stability and Growth Pact
SMP	Securities Markets Program
SPV	Special Purpose Vehicle
SRF	Single Resolution Fund
SRM	Single Resolution Mechanism
SSM	Single Supervisory Mechanism
TLTRO	Targeted Longer-Term Refinancing Operations
UBS	Unemployment Benefit Scheme

VAT	Value Added Tax
QE	Quantitative Easing

Table of Graphs

Graph 1: Nominal Unit Labor Costs (1999=100; per person; total economy) 19

Graph 2: Real Unit Labor Costs (1999=100; per person; total economy) 21

Graph 3: Average inflation rates (GDP deflator), 2000-2008 22

Graph 4: Real Labor Productivity (per person, 1999=100) 22

Graph 5: Total R&D expenditure (in % of GDP) 23

Graph 6: Current Account Balance (in % of GDP) 24

Graph 7: Consolidated Gross National Debt (in % of GDP) 25

Graph 8: Annual government deficit (in % of GDP) 25

Graph 9: Ten-year government bond rates 26

Graph 10: Ten-year government bond rates 35

Graph 11: Consolidated Gross National Debt (in % of GDP) 35

Graph 12: Domestic sovereign debt holdings of MFIs as a percentage of total assets 44

Graph 13: Inflation rate (Annual average rate of change; All-items HICP; Euro area 19) 51

Graph 14: ECB interest rates and the overnight interest rate (percentages per annum) 52

Graph 15: Gross Domestic Product (at market prices; chain linked volumes, index 2010=100) 61

Graph 16: Real Unit Labor Costs (1999=100) 71

Graph 17: Average inflation rates (GDP deflator), 2010-2016 72

Graph 18: Current Account Balance (in % of GDP) 72

Graph 19: Real Labor Productivity (per person, 1999=100) 73

Graph 20: Total R&D Expenditure (in % of GDP) 74

1 Introduction

„If the Euro fails, Europe fails"
Angela Merkel, German Chancellor (2010).

When Chancellor Merkel (Deutscher Bundestag 2010) emphasized the paramount importance of the Monetary Union for Europe with the above sentence in 2010, she intended to justify rescue measures to the extent of hundreds of billions of Euros to safe the eurozone. Albeit it may be controversial to link the future of a whole continent to the persistence of a currency, it is rather unequivocal that major efforts were necessary to prevent the break-up of the euro area. Eventful years have passed by since then, with countless seeming crisis summits, reform efforts that did not yield the desired success, political conflicts, social turmoil, emerging anti-Euro parties and crisis peaks in 2012 and 2015 that created existential problems. The collapse of the eurozone could be averted and progress on stabilizing the euro area was made as well. Some of the countermeasures, however, led to disagreements and fierce criticism. Moreover, it is clear that the adjustments of the Euro's architecture are insufficient and partially of a provisional nature.

Even though there is a consensus that more reforms have to be implemented to base the Monetary Union on a solid, well-functioning fundament ensuring that future shocks do not bring the whole system to the brink of the abyss, no agreement for a large-scale redesign was found yet. This is due, among other things, to the fact that in the current political and social environment it is rather difficult to find a solution that is both expedient and agreeable. Nonetheless, a way out of the crisis must be found and, in fact, many proposals have been contributed in order to do so. The objective of this thesis is to review the suggested solutions to find answers to the question "how can the euro area crisis be solved in the long run"?

For the purpose of approaching this question, the following structure shall apply: Before dealing with possible solutions, the design flaws of the Currency Union will be identified in part 2. In order to get a greater understanding of the characteristics of monetary unions, the optimum currency area theory (OCA) will be presented first. Thereby, it will be outlined that countries should fulfill several criteria before sharing a currency. Since the eurozone member states did not meet the requirements, additional regulations were established to ensure that the countries would at least eventually develop into being close to an optimum currency area. However, it will become evident that this plan failed in a sense that the member states economically drifted apart even more after the Euro was introduced. In the aftermath of the World Financial Crisis the outcomes of the adverse divergence process became obvious, but then it was too late to avoid the escalation of the euro area crisis. In various sections it will be analyzed why the surging imbalances could be built up and why the handling of the crisis was so difficult for the European decision-makers. In the course of this analysis it will be detected that economists still have different views on the deeper causes of the crisis and mainly disagree on the question whether the lack of fiscal discipline or the member states' dependency on capital markets behavior was the key driver of the crisis.

In part 3, the countermeasures that have been applied will be listed and grouped in the three categories macroeconomic measures, monetary policy and Banking Union. Afterwards, in a next part, these rescue efforts will be examined more closely to reveal their benefits and possible adverse effects. It will be concluded that the measures were inevitable to prevent the break-up of the eurozone, but that they do not sufficiently remedy the underlying construction faults of the Monetary Union and that some of them should be replaced due to negative implications. This part will be finished with an interim conclusion in which the remaining problems that still need to be tackled will be highlighted.

Part 5 will include a wide selection of proposals that aim at solving one or more of these unresolved design faults. The suggestions will be categorized according to the proposed degree of economic integration. The ones implying further integration steps in the form of an advanced fiscal union or Eurobonds, for instance, will be reviewed first. Thereafter, concepts how to impose more responsibility on the individual governments and to generally eliminate the divergence of control and liability in the euro area will be scrutinized.

Based on the analysis of the crisis origins, the countermeasures, the open issues and the proposed solutions an idea how to reform the Currency Union such that it is finally made viable and more resistant to asymmetric shocks will be developed in part 6. Thereby, a three-part proposal of Corsetti et al. (2016) will be used as reference point. Ultimately, the thesis will be rounded off with a conclusion.

Several limitations have to be made in advance. Some economists and other observers arrive at the insight that it would be the best solution to find an orderly way how to break up the eurozone. There are reasons that justify this argumentation, but in this research paper it is assumed that the continuation of the Euro is the only realistic option. Hence, the disintegration of the Currency Union will not be addressed. Furthermore, it should be stressed that the approach to answering the research question is very comprehensive. Each describing and discussing the roots of the crisis and the counteractions could easily fill a thesis alone. Combining both and adding potential solutions implies that not all details can be illustrated, even though it is intended to cover as many of them as possible.

2 Origins of the euro area crisis

2.1 Theory: Optimum currency areas

The OCA theory explores the costs and benefits of a common currency and establishes criteria that make participating in such a monetary union reasonable. Optimality is defined as the realization of both internal and external balance (Tavlas 2009: 536). There are six criteria that can be divided into three economic and three political points. The first three criteria were contributed by Mundell, McKinnon and Kenen who are considered to be the most important authors from the first, traditional phase of OCA theory (Broz, 2005, p. 59). There was a second phase afterwards with input coming from more authors such as Corden (1972), again Mundell (1973), Ishiyama (1975) and Tower and Willet (1976).

The OCA theory starts from weighing the costs and benefits of sharing a common currency. The advantages of a monetary union are reduction of transaction costs, abolition of currency risk, higher price transparency, enhanced trade and greater competition as prices are easier to compare (Krugman, 2012: 440). By contrast, the main cost arises from the fact that fixed exchange rates or, respectively, a common currency withdraw the exchange rate as an instrument of adjustment from governments (ibid.). This is detrimental in the event of an asymmetric shock or a symmetric shock with asymmetric effects that lowers the export level of a country. In such a case, it would be conventional for a state to react with currency depreciation in order to make its own products cheaper abroad. Due to the fact that this is not possible for members of a currency union, the adjustment process becomes more complicated. In addition, the common central bank carries out a single monetary policy for the whole currency area, which means that it aligns its interest rates to the economic conditions of all member states (Baldwin, Wyplosz 2015: 359). In the event of an asymmetric shock it is likely to set the interest rates according to the average which is neither perfectly suitable for the affected nor the unaffected countries (ibid.).

The state hit by the shock must then restore competitiveness by lowering prices and/or wages (Eichengreen 1990: 143). However, this is a painful process and if prices and wages fail to decline significantly, unemployment results. The amount of the costs depends on the extent of the asymmetric shocks that hit a currency union member state and the ease with which the affected economy is able to adjust (Maes 1992: 147). This ability of adjusting is examined in the OCA theory and depends on the following six criteria.

2.1.1 The six criteria of OCA theory

The first criterion, factor mobility, was contributed by Mundell in 1961 (Ibid.: 138). Mundell (1961: 958-659) discovered that it becomes less cumbersome to deal with asymmetric shocks when the factors of production, capital and labor, can be moved easily across borders. A given factor mobility would enable a country that experiences a negative demand shock and a subsequent increase in unemployment to shift labor and capital to another member state with higher demand and inflationary pressure. The argument seems valid, but three critical points should be mentioned (Baldwin, Wyplosz 2015: 363). Firstly, cultural and linguistic differences complicate the relocation of workers across borders. Secondly, produced goods may differ from country to country; hence it would take some time to retrain the employees until they can start working effectively. Finally, workers need equipment to be productive. Shifting labor from one country to another could fail because of insufficient means of production in the absorbing state. Labor is mobile as well as financial capital, but plants and equipment cannot be easily relocated. Thus, it can be concluded that even if labor was mobile, it could take years to create the necessary framework. By then, the asymmetric shock may be over anyway.

The second criterion was first stated by McKinnon in 1963 and deals with the openness of a country. McKinnon concentrated, unlike Mundell, on the goods markets and on the conditions which make exchange rate adjustments ineffective (Maes 1992: p. 145). He divided economies into tradable and non-tradable goods sectors and linked the openness of a country to its share of tradables (Ishiyama 1975: 349-350). By arguing that domestic currency prices of tradable goods would change to a more or less equal extent when an open economy uses exchange rate adjustments to correct external deficits, he concluded that countries that heavily trade with each other are rather compatible to form a currency union (Broz 2005: 57). Baldwin and Wyplosz (2015: 365), however, object that the trend towards international value chains makes the criterion less relevant as imported components become more expensive when the currency is depreciated.

Six years after McKinnon had published his ideas, Kenen (1969: 65) introduced the third criterion which consists of product diversification and similar production structures. He claimed that a country with a well-diversified production sector will not face strong asymmetric shocks in the first place since there will be export losses and successes, but the aggregated level will be more or less constant. Thus, product diversification would forestall the need for modifications in terms of trade through the exchange rate, thereby making a state more suitable to a currency union (Tavlas 2009: 539). Furthermore, Kenen pointed out that if countries have a similar production structure, a sector-specific shock was likely to affect them equally. Again, this would qualify them for sharing a common currency (ibid.). Yet, it should be noted that the exact level of required diversification is hard to determine (Baldwin, Wyplosz 2015: 364).

It was also Kenen who recognized that if an asymmetric shock hits a currency union, fiscal integration between the member states can mitigate the effects through fiscal transfers (Broz 2005: 59). This view was shared by Mundell who published two new scientific papers in the early 1970s. He (1973: 115) came to the conclusion that "the use of a common currency (or foreign exchange reserves) allows the country to run down its currency holdings and cushion the impact of the loss, drawing on the resources of the other country until the cost of the adjustment has been effectively spreads over the future". This was tantamount to a paradigm shift, since only a decade before he had posited that labor mobility was confined to rather small national or regional domains which is why countries would be well-advised to maintain an independent monetary policy (McKinnon 2015: 451). As it will be discussed later, fiscal transfers between member states of a monetary union are highly controversial since they can provoke moral hazard. Given a subsequent misbehavior of governments, shocks would not be random and transfers would not balance out but have a permanent direction (Baldwin, Wyplosz 2015: p. 366).

The fifth criterion deals with the political dimension and highlights that a high degree of homogeneity is vital within a monetary union (Torres 2008: 63). According to this reasoning, asymmetric shocks would provoke conflicts if the member states' preferences were too heterogeneous, since countermeasures often require a consensus. An example would be the single monetary policy of a shared central bank. Baldwin and Wyplosz (2015: 366-367) criticize the unspecific character of this statement and advert to the fact that disagreements are normal in politics, even within a country.

The sixth and final criterion refers to the interstate relationships. When the adjustment possibilities, the level of homogeneity of production structures, consumption patterns and openness to trade are insufficient, solidarity may help to keep a monetary union sustainable (Torres 2009: 63). Since none of the criteria is likely to be fully satisfied, asymmetric shocks will always cause political disagreement regarding the correct response. This is a normal feature in any country where solidarity among the citizens contributes to the acceptance of the resulting solution of a debate and the bearing of costs. Occasional costs from asymmetric shocks should be more than compensated by benefits of a common currency. However, if the benefits are too diffuse to be fully observable solidarity becomes essential (Baldwin, Wyplosz 2015: 367). This supports the viewpoint that monetary unions can only emerge after a political union which implies the necessary solidarity among the member states. In any case, the past years have shown that the issue of solidarity can be a very narrow tightrope walk.

After the two waves in the 1960s and 1970s there was a slowdown in research about OCA theory, most probably there were no practical examples of currency unifications (Broz 2005: 61-62). In the 1990s, OCA theory received a new boost as the European Monetary Union (EMU) was to come. Modern OCA theory set new topics on the agenda, such as effectiveness of monetary policy, correlation and variation of shocks and synchronization of business cycles. However, as the new insights play a less important role for the research question of this thesis as well as for reasons of space, the modern views on OCA theory will not be examined.

2.1.2 Did the eurozone fulfill the OCA requirements?

Naturally, the question arises whether the member states of the euro area met the conditions of OCA theory. As pointed out before, countries most likely do not meet the criteria to the full extent and, as a matter of course, theory can never perfectly reflect and predict reality. Nevertheless, in the present context it is helpful to evaluate the countries' qualification to enter the eurozone according to the OCA benchmarks. Again, due to lack of space, it is not possible to carry out a detailed analysis for each country. However, reviewing literature yields a rather clear outcome in this respect anyway: in the years before and when introducing the Euro, the participating European states were far from forming an optimum currency area (Frankel 2015b: 110).

Fuest and Becker (2017: 109) state that three points were most relevant for the eurozone. First of all, a high level of openness and integration, which was given due to the European Single Market. Secondly, product diversification as well as homogeneity of the production structure was existent or, put differently, at least not worse than in the USA. As third aspect, Fuest and Becker mention adjustment mechanisms which include labor mobility and fiscal transfers. Here, most economists (cf. Stiglitz 2017: 11, Scharpf 2011: 325 or Baldwin, Wyplosz 2015:

370-371) agree that the euro area member states exhibited major defects from the very beginning. Cross-border labor mobility was low, labor markets were rigid and interregional transfers were almost completely missing. Moreover, the countries were very heterogeneous with regard to their economic structures therefore also their growth and inflation dynamics.

Additionally, Baldwin and Wyplosz (2015: 374-375) discuss the remaining criteria and deduce that preferences, for example in terms of inflation rates or public debt, were and are rather heterogeneous. They postulate that this is reducible to the fact that policy-making institutions differ from country to country with respect to the roles of executive and parliament or the influence of trade unions. With reference to solidarity, they infer that it is exceedingly difficult to measure this criterion.

2.2 Design flaws in the EMU

2.2.1 Convergence criteria and further rules

In the previous part, it became evident that the countries that opt for sharing the Euro as common currency did not adequately fulfill the OCA criteria and thus were not really compatible for creating a monetary union. Apart from that, it is worth remarking that not only economists then and now were in agreement about the shortcomings, but also European decision-makers were aware of the deficiencies. The founding fathers of the eurozone knew that the fiscal, financial and monetary institutions were not sufficiently developed for a sustainable currency union in Europe (Corsetti 2015: 85). Yet, the politics was not strong enough to implement powerful institutions that would have been necessary to make the Euro a successful project right from the start (Stiglitz 2017: 11). Consequently, the politicians decided to proceed in gradual phases in order to achieve a convergence of the financial and economic capability of the individual member states (Riehle 2016: 20-21). Additionally, by implementing further rules it should be prevented that the incompleteness of the eurozone's architecture would have dire effects. However, the European countries could only agree on the lowest common denominator and were left with hoping for the preferences to converge over time such that the required institutions could be created eventually (Bongardt, Torres 2017: 18). One outcome of the negotiations was the establishment of the so-called convergence criteria (or 'Maastricht criteria'). This set of requirements was arranged to ensure that at the beginning the euro area states would have a minimum convergence level, which they were supposed to increase thereafter by continued adherence[1] (Afxentiou 2000: 249). The countries that intended to join the Monetary Union had to commit to (i) having an inflation rate not above 1.5 percentage points of the average of the three member states with the lowest inflation rates, (ii) having a public budget deficit of not more than three percent of its GDP, (iii) having a gross debt-to-GDP ratio of not more than 60%, (iv) having nominal long-term interest rates not exceeding by more than two percentage points the rate of the three best performing member states in terms of price stability, and (v) participating in the European Exchange Rate Mechanism II without large-scale realignments.

Against the backdrop of building the eurozone on a weak fundament, European leaders decided to set up further regulations. In particular, two articles of the Treaty on the Functioning of the European Union should be mentioned in this context. On the one hand, there is Article 123 which prohibits the monetary financing of sovereigns through the European Central Bank (ECB) and thereby guarantees its independency. On the other hand, Article 125, which is better known as the 'no-bail-out clause', was enshrined in the Treaty. Both can be seen as additional pillars of the eurozone's architecture at that time. Their purpose was to produce fiscal discipline among the member states, to ensure price stability in the euro area and to rule out mutual assumption of debt.

2.2.2 Convergence plan, but divergence reality

As described, the imperfect construction of the Currency Union should be compensated by implementing rules and requirements such that the member states could realize the requisite convergence in the years after the Euro was installed. However, as it will be illustrated in this section, this plan failed monumentally.

In fact, not even at the beginning of the Monetary Union all euro states met the convergence criteria (Riehle 2016: 63-64). Belgium and Italy, for instance, should not have been allowed to enter the eurozone due to their high debt levels. While these rule violations were known, other contenders clandestinely distorted their

1 The convergence criteria were integrated into the Stability and Growth Pact (SGP) which was created in 1997 to enhance the monitoring and coordination of the member states' fiscal and economic policies to enforce the deficit and debt thresholds established by the Maastricht Treaty.

numbers in order to fulfill the Maastricht criteria (Winkler 2016: 154-155). Greece was also far from being ready for a European currency and from providing satisfactory economic data (Frankel 2015b: 112). As it was revealed later, Greece handed in its application for membership with falsified statistical specifications; inter alia it whitewashed its debt level with the help of Goldman Sachs (Riehle 2016: 64). After this poor start, the eurozone experienced an enormous economic divergence in its first decade, although the opposite was intended. By means of data, this will be shown in the following.

When analyzing the divergence in the euro area between the introduction of the Euro and the start of the crisis, one inevitably comes across differences in competitiveness. A glance at the corresponding literature, however, leads to the conclusion that the economic competitiveness of a country is a broad concept that is interpreted very differently[2]. In order to provide a robust theoretical and empirical link between drivers of competitiveness and macroeconomic performance, the ECB founded the Competitiveness Research Network (CompNet) in 2012. The network sets a main focus on the micro dimension on the grounds that aggregate performance depends strongly on firm-level decisions (Lopez-Garcia et al. 2014: 4). For the purpose of fostering the debate on competitiveness issues the researchers developed a new database with information on the distribution of labor productivity or unit labor costs for individual industries but also at sector-level or considering the full economy. Their analysis includes a wide-ranging list of indicators such as labor productivity, capital intensity, price-cost margin, equity ratios or firm's total export (Lopez-Garcia, di Mauro 2015: 23). Such an in-depth assessment cannot be given in this thesis, but nonetheless the general conclusion that the

---

2 Porter (1991: 93–97), for example, starts from the basic principle that the competition is between companies, not countries. In his so-called Diamond approach, he points out that both business-strategic concepts and economic conditions are crucial factors for competitiveness. Lawrence (2002) focuses on the general living standard and uses macroeconomic values such as output per worker or income per capita. For Krugman (1994: 37), however, data about total factor productivity is of crucial importance in this context. Schwab and Sala-i-Martin (2014: 4) "[...] *define competitiveness as the set of institutions, policies, and factors that determine the level of productivity of a country*" and provide a twelve-part list of pillars of competitiveness which, among others, includes infrastructure, goods and labor markets efficiency and financial market development. They (2014: 8) point out that notably (technological) innovation is essential for long-run productivity growth and a resulting sufficient competitiveness level. Therefore, they consider investment in research and development (R&D) to be an indispensable requirement.

competitiveness levels diverged significantly in the first decade of the eurozone, a result at which the CompNet arrives as well (Lopez-Garcia et al. 2014: 5), should be substantiated with a selection of data. In the economic discussion, some factors considered essential for the buildup of large intra-eurozone imbalances appear very frequently. That particularly applies to the price and cost competitiveness[3] and thereby includes unit labor costs.

Graph 1 shows the development of the nominal unit labor costs for a selection of eurozone countries that includes both the crisis-ridden states (mainly in the South of Europe) and some of the more stable states of the North. Evidently, the nominal unit labor costs in Greece, Ireland, Portugal, Spain, Italy and Cyprus (the so-called 'GIPSIC' countries) increased tremendously relative to Germany.

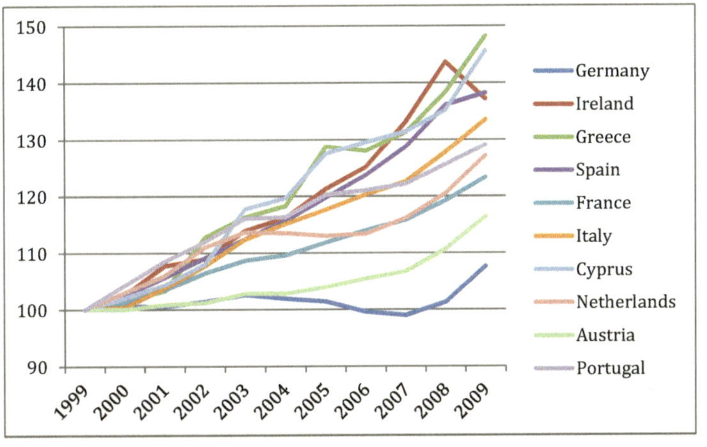

Graph 1: Nominal Unit Labor Costs (1999=100; per person; total economy)
Source: Eurostat, own calculations

However, unit labor costs should be handled with caution. Firstly, former empirical research showed that there is a negative correlation between growth in unit labor costs and output growth (Felipe, Kumar 2011: 3-4). Furthermore, the calculation of unit labor costs can lead to biased findings and arguments can be

3 The ECB calculates Harmonized Competitiveness Indicators (HCIs) in order to evaluate the price or cost competitiveness of the member states relative to their principal competitors (both intra and extra euro area). In this context, they also make use of the GDP deflator and unit labor costs for the total economy which both will be examined in the following.

found that it is not expedient too compare the unit labor costs of the GIPSIC states with those of Germany (ibid.: 5-10).

Bourgeot (2013: 2) agrees with linking common imbalances to divergences in unit labor costs, but objects to the dominant crisis narrative[4] which postulates that the crisis-stricken countries had lived beyond their means or, put more precisely, had experienced a wage drift that had caused their deficits. He (2013: 6-7) claims that looking at nominal unit labor costs is not sufficient to understand the underlying fundamentals of the surge in imbalances. Instead it would be of paramount importance to make a distinction between the different variables that influence nominal unit labor costs and, in particular, to isolate the direct contribution made by inflation.

As illustrated in graph 2, the real unit labor costs indeed deviate from their nominal counterpart. Especially the numbers for Ireland, Spain and Portugal are different. This indicates that differences in inflation played a substantial role during this time period. As a consequence, Bourgeot (2013: 9-11) scrutinizes the member states individually and concludes that low productivity gains and the differing inflations rates were mostly responsible for the divergence in unit labor costs.

4 In Baldwin et al. (2015: 1), for example, declining levels of competitiveness are traced backed to increased public spending which in turn raised the wage level as well as the costs of the respective countries. Riehle (2016: 61) refers to high wage increases in the GIPSIC states as cause for their weak price competitiveness.

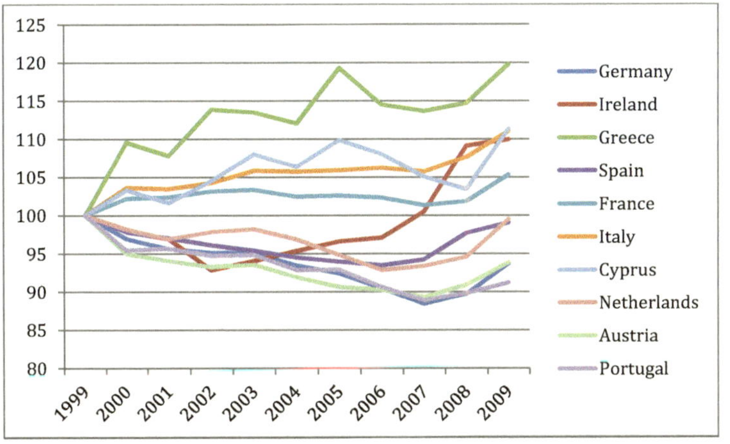

Graph 2: Real Unit Labor Costs (1999=100; per person; total economy)
Source: Ameco, own calculations

Baldwin and Wyplosz (2015: 412-413) also emphasize that permanently higher inflation rates in the peripheral Euro states relative to the core countries[5] promoted the surge of imbalances as their real effective exchange rates (REERs) appreciated accordingly

In this context, it is reasonable to look at the GDP deflator and not the consumer price index (CPI) to check for the inflation differences as the GDP deflator represents the inflation of production and not consumer prices, therefore excluding imports (Bourgeot 2013: 8). In graph 3 it can be seen that Germany was considerably below euro area average in the years before the crisis, while the GIPSIC countries experienced inflations rates above the average[6].

5 In both the literature and the media it is frequently distinguished between peripheral and core countries of the euro area. However, there is no official definition of these terms. The eurozone periphery is mostly equated with the GIPSIC countries, while the core includes Germany, France, the Benelux countries, Finland and Austria. This understanding shall apply for this thesis.

6 In fact, all four state that eventually signed bailout packages, namely Greece, Ireland, Portugal and Spain (see below), had inflation in excess of the average.

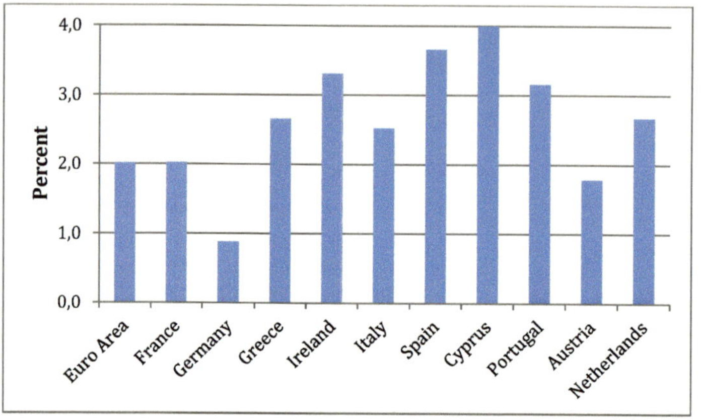

Graph 3: Average inflation rates (GDP deflator), 2000-2008
Source: IMF International Financial Statistics, own calculations

The data on real labor productivity, documented in graph 4, confirms Bourgeot's view that rather inflation rate differences and low productivity gains have been the driving force for competitiveness divergence.

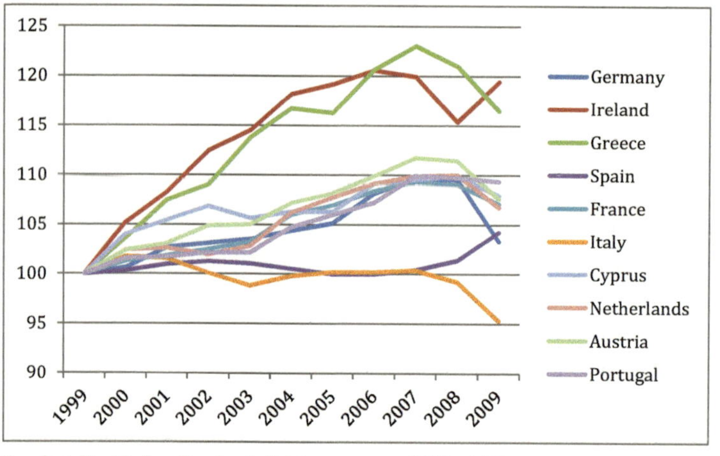

Graph 4: Real Labor Productivity (per person, 1999=100)
Source: Eurostat, own calculations

In regards to Germany, Meloni (2016: 18-19) points out that the exceptional export performance of the German economy was mainly due to the massive wage reduction, but not because of productivity gains. In fact, the productivity development in Germany was rather modest between 1999 and 2009. Meloni continues that, given the restrictive wage policy, especially the manufacturing sector experienced a real devaluation and resulted in a strong decrease in the REER for Germany, while in Southern countries price competitiveness indicators (based on nominal unit wage cost) surged.

Divergences in competitiveness can possibly also be explained by differences in spending in Research and Development, as displayed in graph 5. Naturally, raising funds does not necessarily lead to successful research outcomes and technological innovation. Furthermore, investments in R&D influence the competitiveness only in the medium-to-long term. However, even when pre-euro area years are included it becomes evident that the crisis-ridden states constantly invested less into R&D than the stable countries. This may have contributed to the divergence in competitiveness.

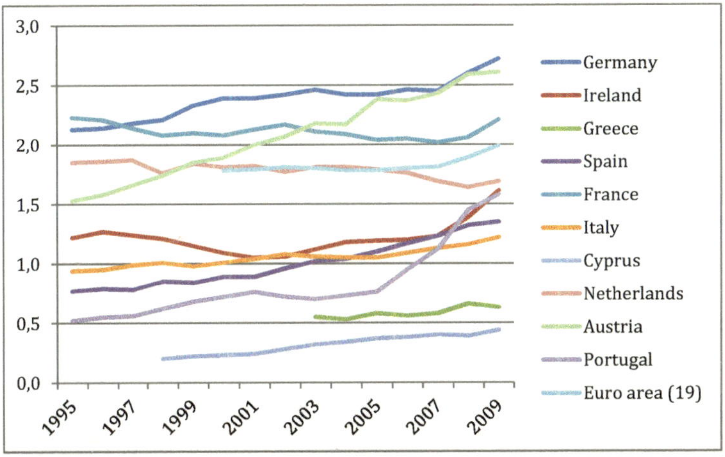

Graph 5: Total R&D expenditure (in % of GDP)
Source: Eurostat

To summarize, it can be difficult to draw conclusions from competitiveness indicators, but in the case of the euro area it seems unambiguous that a divergence of the member states' competitiveness has happened (Feld et al. 2015: 191). Differing trends could also be observed in other areas, as it can be seen in graph 6 which contains the current account balance in percent of GDP of the same selection of countries. It is obvious that Portugal, Greece or Spain had negative numbers already before the introduction of the Euro, but after 1999 or, respectively, 2001 there is a further divergence observable. Apparently, the Northern eurozone countries were net lenders to foreigners while just the opposite was true for the Southern states. Baldwin et al. (2015: 5) identify differences in savings and investments as key driver behind this process[7].

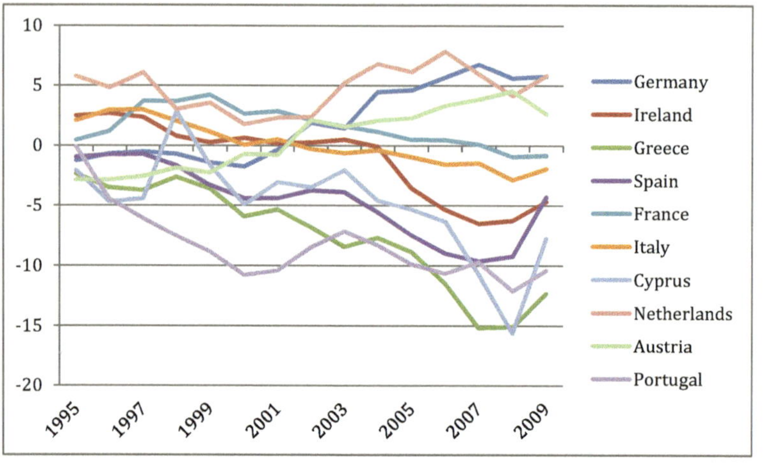

Graph 6: Current Account Balance (in % of GDP)
Source: IMF, WEO database

The combination of eroding competitiveness and negative current account balance developments is likely to result in a large accumulation of debt. Graph 7 illustrates that the euro area countries experienced increasing debt-to-GDP ratios after 2007 which can be related to the World Financial Crisis. Prior to that, the data does not reflect the core-vs.-periphery-structure of the previous categories. Greece and Italy had debt levels far above the 60% debt-to-GDP threshold of the Maastricht Treaty, but this was already the case before the eurozone was brought to life. Particularly worthy of emphasis is that Spain and Ireland, which had to struggle extraordinarily hard during the euro area crisis, were the poster children in the run-up to the crisis with respect to their debt levels.

7 Baldwin et al. provide further data on savings and investments which shows that the GIPSIC countries had below-average savings and tended to overinvest at home. Conversely, core nations such as Germany, the Netherlands, France and Belgium saved above average and tended to underinvest domestically.

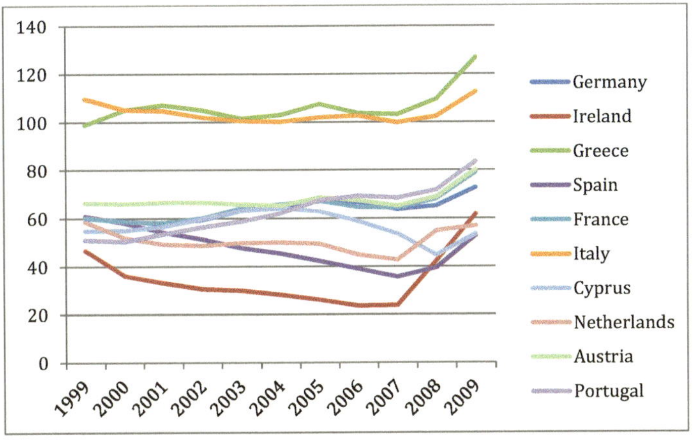

Graph 7: Consolidated Gross National Debt (in % of GDP)
Source: Eurostat

It is also remarkable that Germany, Austria and France, hence less crisis-affected member states, had levels above the allowed threshold and thereby continuously violated this Maastricht criterion. Same holds true for the public budget deficit. Graph 8 indicates that, while Ireland and Spain met their obligations, Greece was constantly far from doing so and that Italy, Portugal, France, Germany, Austria and Cyprus were more than once beyond the 3% limit.

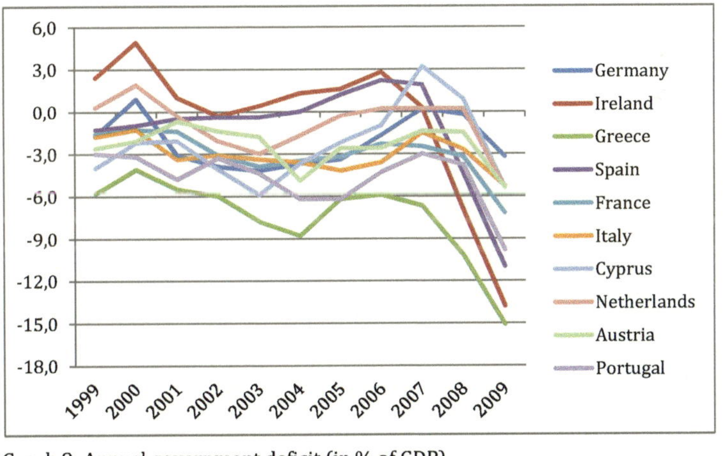

Graph 8: Annual government deficit (in % of GDP)
Source: Eurostat

In summary, it can be said that the plan of the eurozone's architects did not work. Instead of economic convergence, the member states diverged significantly in terms of competitiveness which caused the accumulation of imbalances. The direction of these developments is the same in most cases: the Northern euro area countries experienced competitiveness gains relative to the Southern euro area states and built up current account surpluses while the South run into trade deficits. With regard to the debt and deficit levels, however, the structure is not that clear. Evidently, also stable eurozone sovereigns violated the Maastricht criteria, while both Spain and Ireland which faced huge difficulties during the crisis complied with the rules.

Before starting with the next section, a convergence that actually happened should be mentioned. The interest rates on sovereign bonds with a ten years maturity markedly converged shortly prior to the introduction of the Euro and followed similar movement patterns thereafter. This becomes apparent in graph 9. Consequently, the borrowing costs were significantly lowered, both for private and sovereign borrowers (Baldwin et al. 2015: 3)[8]. Drops in refinancing costs were particularly large in Italy, Portugal, Spain and Greece. The Italian government, for instance, had to pay an interest rate of 12.21% in 1995 and only 4.73% four years later.

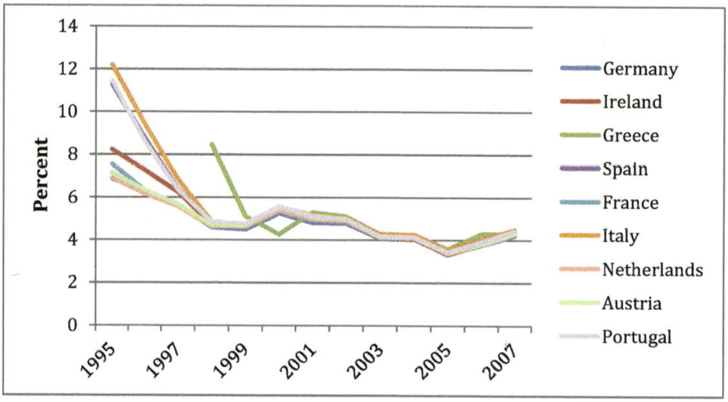

Graph 9: Ten-year government bond rates
Source: OECD database

8 Baldwin et al. point to the fact that interest rates not only fell in European countries, but also in other advanced economies such as the USA, the UK and Japan. However, they still relate the drop of borrowing costs in Europe to the capital markets' anticipation of the Monetary Union.

2.2.3 How was the divergence possible?

In the last section, it was explained that the planned convergence in the eurozone did not happen, but that the member states economically moved apart from each other instead. Naturally, this begs the question how this development could emerge. However, before examining the reasons for the divergence, two limitations have to be made. First of all, the economic development of a country depends not only on the framework of the currency it uses, but on various micro- and macroeconomic factors and decisions made by politicians, private households, companies, capital market participants, and so on. Since a detailed, country-specific analysis cannot be given here, the focus is put on design flaws at eurozone level and less on national conditions.

Secondly, when attempting to find answers to the question why the member states diverged, one starts delving into the causes for the euro area crisis. As a matter of fact, there are rather proximate and rather deep causes. Especially with regard to the deeper, underlying roots of the crisis, economists are still divided by disagreement and each scientific contribution claims prerogative of interpretation of the facts and data. It is in the nature of things that the results of a root cause analysis essentially influence the ensuing solution finding. However, there is neither a consensus on how to interpret the divergences and imbalances nor on the underlying causes. Accordingly, as it will be pointed out later, opinions on how to stabilize the euro area are (therefore) deeply divided as well[9].

False start: false theory, false initial conversion rates

Looking backwards, the decision to implement the Euro on such a weak fundament nearly seems surprising today. Therefore, in order to understand the background of the eurozone's construction, one needs to be aware of the fact that the creation of the Euro was a political decision in the first place. European political decision-makers knew about the shortcomings (see above) and were warned by several economists[10]. However, they decided to accomplish the

9 It should be noted that, in a broader sense, two opposing views exist whose advocates disagree on the causes and, by implication, on the expediency of the countermeasures that were carried out so far as well as on how to stabilize the euro area. In the course of this thesis, it will be clarified which arguments are urged by both sides with respect to these subject areas.

10 In 1992, a group of 60 economists teamed up and formulated a declaration in which they argued that the introduction of the Euro was premature and would lead to severe economic

Currency Union in an early, imperfect stage. Prior to that, two conflicting theoretical approaches had been discussed. One side argued that the Euro should be the last step of European integration and be based on a political union which should be established first (Fuest, Becker 2017: 29). This view, also known as "coronation theory", was mainly shared by the former German Chancellor Helmut Kohl and the German Central Bank. The opposing side, by contrast, found that the Euro should sooner rather than later be introduced and form the beginning of an evolving European integration with the objective of building a political union. Supporters of this viewpoint assumed that shocks would hit the eurozone and disclose the shortages, but expected the conflicts to be manageable due to the historical importance of the Monetary Union (Corsetti 2015: 86). This opinion is reflected in a statement of Jean Monnet who once wrote that "Europe will be forged in crises, and will be the sum of the solutions adopted for those crises" (Barroso 2011). Another argument was that currency unions tend to increase trade among its members and thereby raise the symmetry of shocks. Hence, a monetary union may develop into meeting OCA criteria ex post even if it does not ex ante (Frankel 2015b: 111).

Clearly, the latter vision prevailed and the Euro was created in the absence of a political union. Fuest and Becker (2017: 29) indicate that the French side put pressure on Germany since the strong German Central Bank was annoying for France as its leading status in the European financial system restricted the French monetary policy. The German government conceded as the Kohl era was nearing its end and the opposition was more and more skeptical about the Euro. The German political leaders did not want to miss on the historical opportunity to foster the European integration and also to win the French government over for the German reunification (ibid.: 32). Nonetheless, political preferences differed and hence the individual objectives: while Germany, Austria, Netherlands and Finland sought for low inflation rates, France and Italy expected economic-stimulating policies from the ECB (ibid.: 36). For this reason, France insisted on Italy, Spain and Portugal to be founding members of the Monetary Union in order to shift the political equilibrium of the eurozone towards France (Riehle 2016: 63-64). Moreover, taking Belgium, which clearly did not fulfill the requirements, in

problems. In fact, the euro area experienced serious difficulties; however, in a different way than it was forecasted (Plickert 2017).

the Currency Union was purely politically motivated as there was a consensus that they could not be left out as founding members of the European Economic Community (ibid.).

Maybe it was just bad luck that the first crisis was of such a large extent as the Great Recession in 2009 (Corsetti: 2015: 86). Possibly, a smaller crisis with less negative impacts had brought the eurozone on the right track. From a today's perspective, however, it appears obvious to conclude that it would have been the better choice to postpone the implementation of the euro area and to improve conditions first. At least, starting the euro area with twelve member states seems to be a wrong decision which caused that Monnet's rationale was eventually turned on its head.

The divergence was also promoted by economic misjudgments: when exchanging the national currencies for the Euros, the initial conversion rates were miscalculated (Baldwin, Wyplosz 2015: 413). For instance, the German conversion rate was too high, while the Greek one was undervalued (Scharpf 2011: 327). Consequently, this contributed to the diverging competitiveness.

Ineffective (public) Debt control and macroeconomic supervision

So evidently, by ignoring economic principles, politicians based the eurozone on false assumptions. Yet, as mentioned before, the politicians realized that the start of the Euro was ill-fated and therefore wrote down strict rules in the Maastricht Treaty. Accordingly, it must be asked why there was a lack of corrections of the undesirable developments over time. The simple answer to this question is that the agreements were breached without entailing serious consequence for the rule breakers, but naturally it is reasonable to look more precisely at this issue.

In order to get a better understanding, it is necessary to begin with the economic situation in the euro area shortly after the turn of the millennium. While the implementation of the Monetary Union and the subsequent decrease in borrowing costs triggered a boom in the peripheral member states[11], France and particularly Germany experienced the opposite: due to the low inflation rates, the real interest rates increased and were followed by a recession (Illing 2017: 16). Additionally, by being oriented at the euro area average, the single monetary policy reinforced this process (Scharpf 2011: 326). Correspondingly, deficits rose

---

11 Except for Cyprus which entered the eurozone in 2008.

above the allowed threshold which prompted the European Commission to initiate a deficit procedure against the French as well as the German government. However, the economic downturn in both states had put strong domestic political pressure on the respective governments. The German Chancellor Gerhard Schröder introduced the controversial Hartz4 reforms to restore competitiveness, and, similar to his French equivalent Jacques Chirac, faced decreasing popularity. Thus, they opposed the deficit procedures and obtained that they were not sanctioned which, from an economic perspective, was not understandable as the deficits were not high and could have been dealt with easily (Fuest, Becker 2017: 39-41). Either way, instead of introducing corrective measures, Germany and France ensured that the rules could be interpreted more flexible from then on[12]. The budgetary control became a plaything of political coalitions afterwards, causing the SGP to fail at being a satisfactory fiscal disciplinary instrument: Sanctions were not imposed as the European Commission was constantly confronted with national arguments of special circumstances (Bongardt, Torres 2017: 18). Moreover, when the member states received reminders from Brussels to comply with the debt rules, they argued that strong future growth would eventually help out. Hence, they modified their GDP forecasts such that future growth rates would compensate for today's deficits, but without adjusting its actual policies (Frankel, Schreger 2013: 248).

The case for the macroeconomic imbalances that were built up is different. Due to the lack of any common policy framework to coordinate national fiscal policy, there was no appropriate cyclical management at eurozone level (Corsetti 2015: 86). The eurozone's architecture did not contain a mechanism that could stop divergent economic developments among its member states (de Grauwe 2015: 100). European politicians did not take the increasing current account imbalances into consideration which is why there was no policy framework for identifying goods imbalances, when capital was shifted into the country because markets had rationally identified market opportunities (Stiglitz 2017: 15). Besides the absence of an institution that could have monitored and regulated the growing imbalances, the divergence in this respect was not interpreted as a problem in the first place. Baldwin et al. (2015: 12-13) note that it was not understood correctly

---

[12] See European Council (2005): Presidency Conclusions: One 'improvement' of the SGP was to "*take better account in Council recommendations of periods when economies are growing below trend*" (2005: 23).

what the oversized capital flows were financing and that they could lead to a crisis. Back then, they were rather seen as a feature of the currency unification and a convergence process.

Despite the temporal distance, economists today still disagree on how to evaluate the debt and trade imbalances that were built up during that time. The prevalent view is that after the introduction of the Euro, the Southern states demanded more credit since the interest rate spreads disappeared (Illing 2017: 16). Due to the declining interest rates, the demand for consumption goods and real estate funded by loans surged and resulted in high growth rates as well as declining unemployment. However, this development was flanked by increasing real wages and unit labor costs, which then led to more imports and current account deficits in the respective countries (Bongardt, Torres 2017: 20). Sinn (2014: 9) adds that the artificial and inflationary growth created by the enhanced borrowing in the GIPSIC states covered up the resulting debt problem for many years. In his opinion, the excessive accumulation of debt led to over-heating economies and consequently moderate debt-to-GDP ratios, while the underlying development of decreasing competitiveness had to let this house of cards fall eventually. For Italy, Baldwin and Wyplosz (2015: 415) arrive at the insight that the windfall gains from lower borrowing costs were not used to reduce the high debt level, but to increase public spending in many areas[13].

The opposing side does not neglect the lower borrowing costs and increasing imbalances, but points to the fact that Ireland and Spain had exemplary debt levels (see section 2.2.2.) before they turned into problematic cases during the crisis. Simultaneously, Germany violated the debt rules, but did not go through an escalating recession. Thus, referring to a solid or irresponsible budgetary policy in the run-up to the crisis would be inappropriate to explain why a state is a creditor or debtor today. Scharpf (2011: 330) therefore concludes that the current account balances were far more essential than the debt levels. Baldwin et al. (2015: 5-6) stress that only Portugal (starting low) and Greece (starting already high) had a sharp increase of their debt-to-GDP ratios between 2000 and 2007.

---

13 Piller (2014) even stresses that the former Italian President, Carlo Azeglio Ciampi, who was involved in the negotiations about the Italian entry to the euro area, speaks of "betrayal" by his successors who did not carry forward the consolidation and reform path Italy had promised to the other member states in exchange for immediate access to the Monetary Union.

They (2015: 12) arrive at the crushing verdict that even countries that had complied with the rules of the SGP got into trouble and so the SGP failed even when its obligations were met.

Both sides provide valid arguments which make it difficult to come to a conclusion. Hence, it might be helpful to include country-specific facts into the analysis. Fuest and Becker (2017: 99-100) claim that one-sided capital flows do not form a problem as such, but rather are a benefit of open markets. Current account imbalances only would be burdening when the capital income is not used for productive investments. Following this logic, it becomes pivotal to examine how the sovereign funds were allocated by the governments. Feld et al. (2016) state that, for instance, in Greece and Portugal increased public lending was not used for productivity- or capacity-enhancing investments. Further indication can be drawn from the so-called cepDefault-index which measures the ability of a country to repay its credits and thereby the development of the creditworthiness. The index is based on the level of capacity enhancing capital formation[14] and the net lending or borrowing of the total economy of a country (Gerken et al. 2017: 2). For the case of Greece, the authors identify a negative trend mainly driven by excessive consumption relative to the euro area average between 2000 and 2009, which led to a high demand for foreign credit (ibid. 2017: 13). Moreover, they state that excessive consumption and too few capacity-increasing investments lowering the Italian creditworthiness (ibid.: 15). Their results for Portugal confirm the assessment of Feld et al. that the Portuguese government did not invest productively enough. According to Gerken et al. (2017: 18-19), there was a combination of significantly declining investments, net borrowing and above-average consumption between 2000 and 2009. Their data for Spain is more positive: the capacity-increasing investments have been high until 2008 while consumption levels were below the average. However, the Spanish economy has been a net capital importer during this time, with deteriorating numbers since 2004 (ibid.: 24). In comparison to this, Germany, Austria or the Netherlands

[14] As explained in Gerken et al. (2017: 3), capacity-increasing investments in this context include both private and public net capital investments, excluding real estate investments since housing construction does not lead to an expansion of the production potential. If a positive value for the capacity increasing investments can be identified for a certain period, it means that during this time additional production potential is created. The value creation of this production potential can later be used to redeem foreign loans. If capacity increasing investments, however, are negative, then the creditworthiness of a country is likely to erode.

performed markedly better with continuous positive capacity-increasing spending and financing balance numbers (ibid.: 29-34). It is somewhat surprisingly, however, that Ireland invested at a high rate, had rather balanced capital imports and exports and consumed clearly below the eurozone average (Gerken et al. 2016: 16-17).

This requests another explanatory approach in the case of Ireland, as well as to some extent for Spain. In fact, the private sector played a key role in these countries and should therefore be analyzed. In both member states large capital inflows were followed by a housing boom and price inflation that was based on an excessive credit expansion (Corsetti 2015: 89). The main problem was the magnitude of the potential liabilities from banks' losses, which became large prospective debt and deficit for the governments (ibid.: 90). For Balwin et al. (2015: 6) the excessive lending activities, especially in Ireland, but also in Spain, should be used to explain the rapid worsening of the respective economic conditions. As much of the lending went into the housing sectors, real estate bubbles emerged. Even though there was empirical evidence that private sector misconduct could lead to an economic crisis, neither the ECB nor the governments tackled this problem (Stiglitz 2017: 15). Eventually, the Irish government had to bail out its oversized banking sector which largely contributed to its deteriorating fiscal situation during the crisis (Frankel 2015a: 430-431). From a today's perspective, it can be noted that the absence of a mechanism to systemically detect and correct private sector imbalances was a crucial weakness of the eurozone's architecture. It was assumed that creditors would impose sufficient discipline, but capital markets did not price public debts accordingly and allowed private imbalances and debts to reach extremely high levels (Bongardt, Torres 2017: 18-19).

The country-specific analysis indicates that in Spain and Ireland, for example, national developments have been highly influential, while for Portugal and Greece the dominant narrative seems to be correct[15].

[15] This reading is reinforced by Blanchard and Giavazzi who already in 2002 referred to growing current account imbalances in Greece and Portugal that had emerged without an adverse economic shock. They (2002: 148-149) reduced this development to the fact that both countries became more closely integrated in goods and financial markets in the euro area. In general, poor countries would provide higher expected rates of return which is why they would experience an increase in investments. Moreover, due to the better growth

2.2.4 World Financial Crisis as trigger and hurdles for the rescue

In any case, the fact that the crisis degenerated into one of existence-threatening extent cannot be explained by only examining the years between the Euro's introduction and the day when the aftermath of Lehman's bankruptcy spread over to Europe. It is essential to bring up that the way the crisis could unfold after 2009, driven by several catalyzers, was of decisive importance for its severity. When the World Financial Crisis started in 2007 in the USA, it took not long until adverse spillover effects were discernible in Europe. Apart from the effects of the US banking and economic crisis, the extreme imbalances in Europe became more and more problematic. Investors reevaluated the creditworthiness of the European states and ceased purchasing sovereign bonds of the Southern countries of the eurozone. This sudden stop of (cross-border) lending led to more concerns about the viability of banks and governments in countries with large current account deficits and dependency on foreign lending[16]. As illustrated in graph 10, risk premiums on government bonds of many Euro states rose tremendously and brought the affected sovereigns into large liquidity problems.

prospects, savings in the poor countries would normally decrease. According to the authors, this decoupling of saving and investment in the eurozone would allow poorer countries to invest more, save less, and run larger current account deficits, while the converse would hold for the richer countries. However, Blanchard's and Giavazzi's (2002: 186) conclusion with regard to policy implications, namely to continue with benign neglect of current account deficits, seems false from a today's viewpoint.

16 Baldwin et al. (2015: 2) emphasize that the crisis in the euro area should be seen as sudden stop crisis that later evolved into a public debt crisis, but categorize the sudden stop of cross-border lending as proximate cause

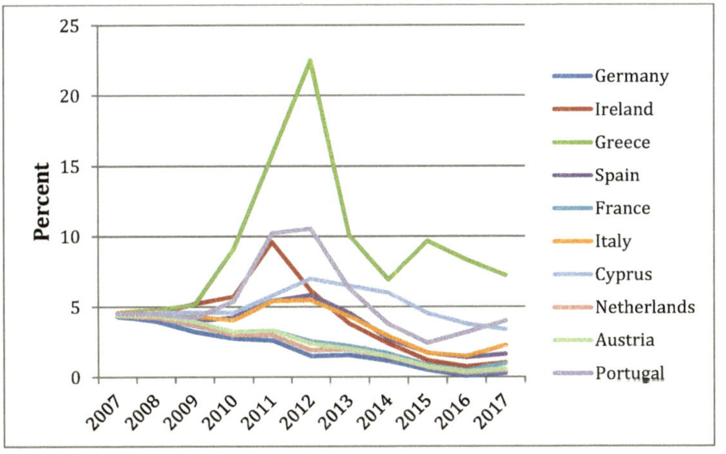

Graph 10: Ten-year government bond rates
Source: ECB Statistical Data Warehouse

Public debt ratios increased rapidly afterwards and threatened the solvency of affected states. Graph 11 shows that the debt-to-GDP ratios reached levels of up to 180% as in the case of Greece. Spain and Ireland which were significantly below the threshold of 60% experienced numbers far beyond this limit within few years.

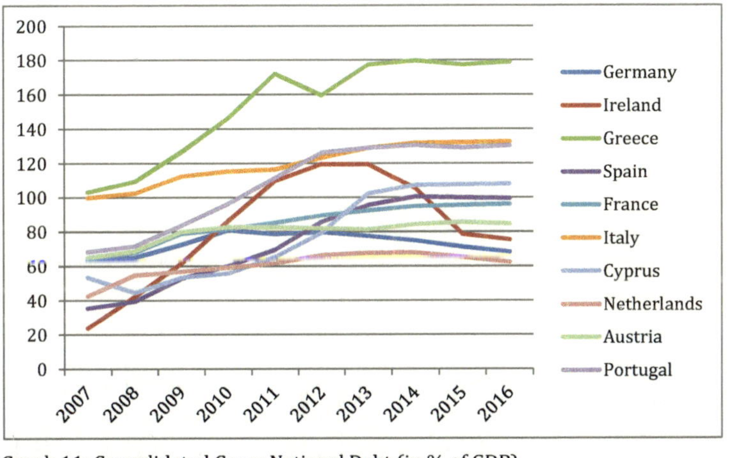

Graph 11: Consolidated Gross National Debt (in % of GDP)
Source: Eurostat

Naturally, it was not the first time in history that an economic crisis and refinancing problems of governments occurred. There are theoretical and practical countermeasures to mitigate the negative effects of an adverse shock.

For the eurozone member states, however, there were several hurdles that made the usage of typical proceedings inaccessible or at least more difficult. These obstacles which largely contributed to the escalation of the crisis will be examined in the next two sections.

The costs of a common currency evolve

The World Financial Crisis hit the eurozone as symmetric shock with asymmetric effects since the sudden stop of foreign lending did not affect all member states. However, being part of a monetary union trimmed the portfolio of standard countermeasures for the respective governments (see section 2.1.). So when the euro area experienced the economic downturn, the costs of sharing a currency unfolded as predicted by OCA theory. Firstly, the crisis-ridden countries could not depreciate the currency (Corsetti 2015: 87-88). Secondly, the ECB was not able to jump in by lowering its interest rates to an adequate level since it found itself in a difficult situation: low interest rates would have been beneficial for the peripheral countries, while they were undesired in the core countries (Riehle 2016: 151-152).

In order to reduce the intra-eurozone imbalances and to restore competitiveness, the member states in crisis had to depreciate internally which required cost reduction through wage and cost moderation (De Grauwe 2015: 100). Unfortunately, restoring competitiveness and reducing debt via wage reduction and cuts in spending are a very painful recovery process for the respective countries (Baldwin, Wyplosz 2015: 491). Unlike currency devaluation, internal depreciation involves low growth rates and rising unemployment (Eichengreen 1990: 143). The alternative of improving competitiveness through productivity-enhancing measures is void since such measures have rather medium-to-long than short-term effects. Moreover, reforms which aim at reducing bureaucracy, opening up professions and liberalizing labor markets are equally unpopular and burdensome (Frankel 2015: 432).

Hence, the classic OCA theoretical arduous conditions cropped up in practice and eminently complicated the crisis management. However, there is more to add. While the interest rate spreads reappeared in the eurozone and caused tremendous refinancing problems for the GIPSIC countries, other highly indebted G7 states such as the USA, Japan or the UK had significantly lower borrowing costs (GCEE 2011: 93). Obviously, the sovereign bonds of these countries were still considered as safe assets. Economists explain the difference with the fact that the other countries have their own central bank which, if necessary, can provide sufficient funds in the event of a liquidity crisis. Thus, liquidity problems do not exist for Japan, the USA or the UK as they get into debt exclusively denominated in their own currency which is why their central banks are always able to generate the money that is needed to repay the debt (ibid.). The case for euro area member states is different: by entering the Currency Union, the member states gave up the Lender of Last Resort (LOLR) function of their central banks which is a fundamental stabilizing instrument (De Grauwe 2015: 103). Consequently, the governments of the eurozone states issued debt denominated in a currency they did not have control over, implying that the sovereigns could not guarantee that they would be capable to carry out the rollover of their debt (GCEE 2015: 39). The founding fathers, however, did not recognize that the inability of states to credibly guarantee the repayment of their debt at maturity could trigger self-fulfilling liquidity crises that could develop into solvency problems (De Grauwe 2015: 103).

Normally, this specific insolvency risk, also referred to as "original sin", is only existent in emerging countries that cannot sell sovereign bonds denominated in their currency on capital markets and thus have to borrow money in a foreign currency (GCEE 2011: 94). While some observers hoped that this mechanism could lead to more fiscal discipline and higher economic competitiveness in the euro area, de Grauwe (2015: 103) concludes that a sudden stop of lending that degenerated into a solvency crisis is exactly what happened in Ireland, Spain and Portugal. Since market participants expected liquidity problems they sold sovereign bonds and thereby raised the interest rate and initiated a liquidity outflow in the affected countries. The increase of interest rates then scaled up the deficit as well as debt levels and pushed governments towards default. De Grauwe and Ji (2013: 17) emphasize that such a development is belief-driven and has a self-fulfilling element in this dynamics: when investors believe that a country might be apart from a sustainable debt path, their actions make it more probable that the respective government indeed fails on debt repayment. In this context, Illing (2017: 19-20) points out that the solvency of a state primarily depends on the relationships among investors. He explains that due to the fact that countries never redeem their debt completely, but roll it over, their creditors must always hope for other financial investors to purchase sovereign bonds of euro area member states. Accordingly, the uncertainty of investors would not be about the relationship between investors and governments, but about trust and expectations among investors themselves. Illing (2017: 21) therefore states that the solvency of euro area countries is determined by capital market participants as well as a government's rating and less by its economic performance, budget deficit or consolidation efforts. Moreover, he (2017: 22-24) finds that due to the fact that governments never repay their debts, the argument of deteriorating competitiveness would be unsound: According to his explanations, investors must have known for years that the economic situation in Greece was disastrous, but still they granted credit to the government even though there were no competitiveness-enhancing investments. Illing (2017: 25) refers to the Outright Monetary Transactions (OMT)[17] program as additional evidence that risk premiums do not reflect the market's opinion on the economic status of a country: Since the OMT program entailed significant lower refinancing costs for the GIPSIC countries, but was not linked to their competitiveness, he argues that the estimated probability of successful repayment would be the decisive factor for the capital market investors.

So broadly speaking, because of the specific insolvency risk some economists attach great importance to capital markets' estimations and intra-investor relationships and find that sovereigns largely depend on the willingness of creditors to continuously lend them money. Following this viewpoint, another issue needs to be raised. The assumption that under the (special) framework of the Monetary Union the market would ensure discipline in the eurozone was already challenged in 1989 by the so-called Delors Report[18]. It was noted that the market's discipline mechanisms would be either too slow and too weak, or too abrupt and too strong (GCEE 2011: 94). Furthermore, empirical data shows that since the beginning of the Currency Union the expectation of the Delors Report that the access to a large capital market could, in the first instance, facilitate the financing of economic imbalances was fulfilled. Hence, the capital market

---

17 The OMT program was a measure implemented by the ECB to prevent the break-up of the eurozone. It was announced that the ECB would purchase sovereign bonds of struggling member states. Thereby, the exorbitant high borrowing costs decreased. More detail is provided in part 3.

18 The Delors Report of 1989, named after the former President of the European Commission Jacques Delors, was a study which was later taken as basis for the Maastricht Treaty. It was made by an expert group which examined the circumstances of the creation of the EMU (Verdun 1999: 308).

participants did not sufficiently evaluate the solvency of the Euro states in the first decade of the Monetary Union (ibid.).

In this respect, two theoretical approaches collide. On the one side there is the fundamentalist view that relates the increase in yield spreads to serious deterioration in states' macroeconomic fundamentals (Saka et al. 2014: 1-2). On the other side there is the multiple-equilibriums view which assumes that markets' evaluations are not always correct and thus countries may be pushed in any one of a set of potential equilibrium conditions, even though fiscal fundamentals did not change. As a consequence, panic-driven investors can trigger a self-fulfilling crisis that otherwise would not have unfolded. In this case, the affected member states were forced into a bad equilibrium characterized by high risk premiums, the need for austerity measures and a deep recession (De Grauwe, Ji 2013: 17). By contrast, countries that experience trust by financial markets receive capital inflows that lower the interest rate and foster the economy, thereby shifting these states in a good equilibrium. According to the multiple-equilibriums view, changes in market sentiments often do not reflect the creditworthiness of a nation, but may lead to large swings in yield differentials and credit rationing (Gros, Mayer 2010). If financial markets make decisions based on irrational sentiments, they certainly do not accurately impose fiscal discipline. In fact, de Grauwe and Ji (2013: 32-33) provide empirical evidence that the Euro states were hit by the sovereign debt crisis due to time dependent negative market sentiments that amplified since the end of 2010. They postulate that the increase of interest rate spreads in the Southern Euro states (except for Greece) was disconnected from surges in the debt-to-GDP ratios and fiscal space in these countries. Moreover, they find that stand-alone countries[19] did not face this kind of liquidity crisis and were not exposed to an increase in the borrowing costs. Thereby, they see their fragility hypothesis validated, meaning that members of a currency union are exposed to such self-fulfilling dynamics of belief-driven speculations.

Saka et al. (2014: 3) add that there is mounting evidence of so-called "wake-up calls", that is, the belief that markets disregard deteriorating fiscal fundamentals in normal times, but become very sensitive to them in crises. From their perspective, fundamentals only have a crucial impact when they reach drastic

[19] Countries that have their own central bank.

dimensions, hence when debt-to-GDP ratios are in a very good or very bad condition. So they do not deny that financial market participants became more sensitive towards fundamentals during the crisis, but for them this does not explain why the euro area states experienced a stronger rise in spreads relative to stand-alone countries with similar fiscal positions[20]. De Grauwe and Ji (2013: 33) conclude that in the case of eurozone member states investors are less tolerant towards public debt accumulation than in countries with an own currency.
It needs to be highlighted that the debate on this argumentation is still ongoing and that there is disagreement among economic researchers. For many economists, fundamentals do play a crucial role for a country's ability to maintain access to the capital markets. They point to the fact that in Portugal, for example, the debt-to-GDP ratio was bad already before 2010. Exploring the details of this discussion could easily fill a whole thesis and cannot be accomplished here, but it is important to understand the main features of the issue since it certainly has decisive impacts on the solution finding.

The lack of a rescue architecture and conflicts of interest

From the very beginning, the Euro was designed as one-way road, meaning that the statutory framework did neither include an exit procedure for a member state nor an insolvency mechanism for the event of public bankruptcy (Baldwin, Wyplosz 2015: 507-508). This was due to two reasons: on the one hand the Euro should constitute a major step of political integration and, to put it in an exaggerated nutshell, was equated with the question of war and peace (Fuest, Becker 2017: 225). Leaving the Monetary Union should thus not be an option. On the other hand, it was assumed that the member states would not get into the situation of facing bankruptcy as they had to comply with the rules of the SGP. When the crisis emerged with its asymmetric character, the affected countries could not resort to a well-conceptualized, functioning rescue architecture as there were no such institutions or procedures.

De Grauwe (2013: 2-3) emphasizes that booms and busts are normal to economies and have happened repeatedly in history which is why stabilizing

[20] In addition, Saka et al. (2014: 28) believe that there was significant contagion from idiosyncratic Spain-specific bad news that affected other Euro states. Same holds true for herding contagion which came in the form of frequent cross-border clusters of large shocks in the eurozone before the implicit OMT announcement. They interpret their results as empirical evidence for a decoupling of fundamentals and markets' lending behavior.

instruments were established for governments to cope with both. He (2013: 6) criticizes that monetary policy was centralized in the eurozone without implementing a LOLR at euro area level, while economic boosts and shocks continued to happen at national level. Moreover, he points to the absence of European automatic budget stabilizers that would take effect during economic downturns[21]. As a consequence, the political leaders not only had to agree on ad hoc measures to handle the current shocks, but were also obliged to find a consensus on how to prevent and/or deal with future macroeconomic and financial crises (Corsetti 2015: 87). Since it became clear that the necessary measures would undermine the no-bail-out clause, the solution finding process was protracted. Further delay accrued from the fact that all parliaments had to agree with necessary resolutions. Fuest and Becker (2017: 97) add that the eurozone members were not prepared for a crisis since both the finance sector and the public budgets were attuned to positive growth. In general, they deprecate that there were neither rescue institutions nor any kind of fiscal buffers and also no consensus on how to solve the crisis.

The latter point should be further elaborated. Indeed, the political disagreements and conflicts at euro area level are considered to be drivers of the escalation of the economic downswing (Stiglitz 2017: 11). The political leaders of the Monetary Union did not only struggle with implementing solutions that ultimately annulled the no-bail-out clause, but were also impeded because large parts of the Greek debt were hold by French and German banks (Baldwin et al. 2015: 13). Due to the lack of an institutional framework that sets rules of managing solvency crises and that provides a backstop for governments, including the sharing of losses and the enforcement of conditionality, European decision-makers became deeply divided over policy solutions and the distribution of the costs (Corsetti 2015: 90-91). So conflicts among the member states could not be avoided and translated into uncertainty and delays in implementing necessary policy measures. This explains, among other things, why the USA reacted more rapidly to the World Financial Crisis (Stiglitz 2017: 12). Discrepancy

---

21 As described earlier, de Grauwe supports the multiple equilibriums view which is opposed by other economists. Calling for automatic stabilizers and a LOLR (e.g. the ECB) on European level is, at least partially, based on the assumption that euro area member states are exposed to belief-driven speculative attacks. This should be kept in mind when referring to them as cause for the eurozone crisis.

was also perceptible between the populations. The whole debate on how to find a way out of this European misery became more and more emotional[22] and complicated the consensus building even further.

Diabolic loop and ineffective banking regulation/supervision

In the last section it was already briefly mentioned that holdings in German and French banks' balance sheets hampered the solving of the crisis. In fact, the relationship between the banking sector and the governments constituted a major problem that needs to be examined.

Similar to the fiscal policy competences, the banking regulation and supervision had been kept at the national level after the introduction of the Euro. This proved to be a fatal error since the differing standards and conventions formed a regulation jungle that was virtually impossible to understand (Fuest, Becker 2017: 90). Thus, the consequences of a bank bankruptcy could not be estimated and therefore this option was excluded. Both the set of rules and its enforcement were weak which led to several undesirable developments. A first flaw was that banks were able to take on excessive risks, inter alia by blowing up private lending (Feld et al. 2016: 1-2). Particularly in Spain and Ireland higher equity ratios would have been helpful to cope with the adverse shock. Many banks in the eurozone, however, were thinly capitalized because there was no explicit regulation to prevent the extreme bank leverage that emerged before the crisis[23] (Baldwin et al. 2015: 12). A second shortcoming was that some banks were able to become "too big to fail", that is, being systemically relevant such that a bankruptcy would have dire consequences for the whole economy of the country of origin (Fuest, Becker 2017: 86-87). Thirdly, the close links between eurozone banks and national governments massively amplified and spread the crisis (Baldwin et al. 2015: 2). Here, it is referred to the so-called "diabolic loop" which means the potential for a vicious feedback circle between sovereigns and their

---

22 It could be thought back to Greek demonstrators comparing Chancellor Merkel with Adolf Hitler or the German "Bild" newspaper headlining "Ihr griecht nix von uns!" (Bild 2010).

23 Baldwin et al. (2015: 12) further explain that having an overleveraged banking sector was not only a European, but a worldwide phenomenon of advanced economies. They identify the intellectual climate of the 1990s as the main fault as it was thought that existing micro-prudential rules were sufficient. Hence, national authorities remained responsible for the banks' balance sheets and centralized supervisions, which would have been necessary, were not pursued.

domestic banks. As stated above, oversized and excessively risk-taking banks posed a threat to governments, but the diabolic loop also had effects in the opposite direction: many banks had purchased domestic sovereign bonds, thereby creating a perilous interdependence between the state and the banking sector (Brunnermeier et al. 2012: 2). Due to the lack of a eurozone bank resolution system the governments relied on the banks for the financial means that would be necessary to save them, but vice versa the governments' solvency had a direct impact on the solvency of the banks (Baldwin, Wyplosz: 501-502). Worsening ratings on government bonds meant deteriorating balance sheets for those banks holding large amounts of the respective bonds.

In graph 12 it is illustrated that the home bias problem, starting in 2008, became critical notably during the crisis when banks increased their holdings of domestic sovereign bonds. This development was mainly observable in Portugal, Italy and Spain and caused by various factors.

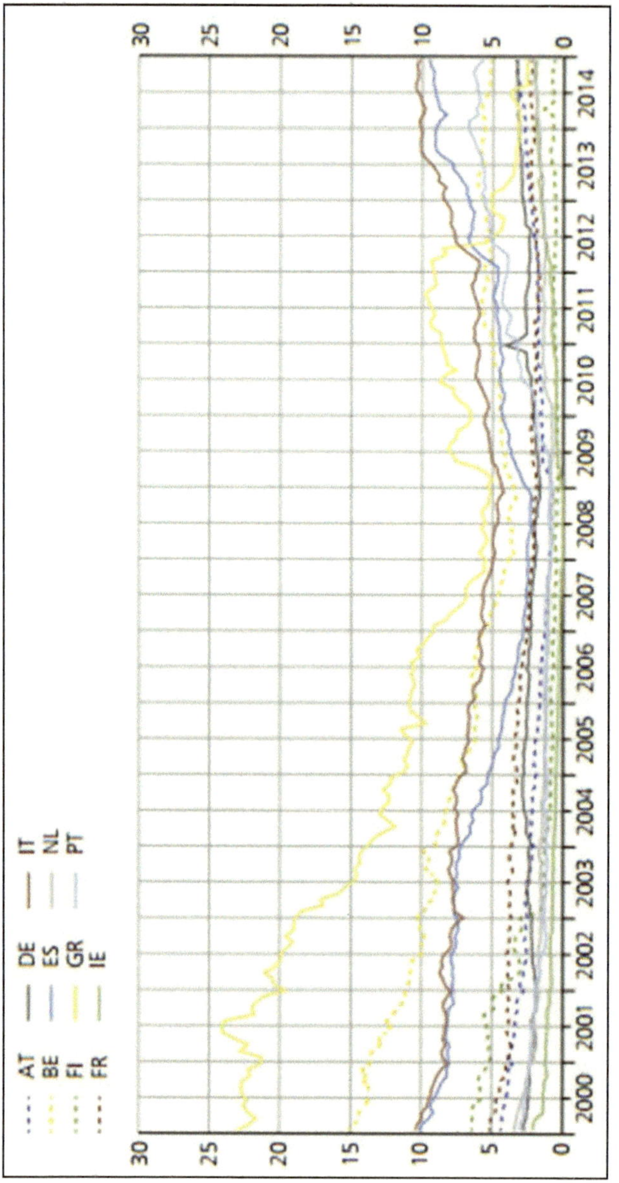

Graph 12: Domestic sovereign debt holdings of MFIs as a percentage of total assets
Source: ESRB report on the regulatory treatment of sovereign exposures (03/2015): p. 79.

Purchasing bonds of peripheral countries while refinancing at the ECB was a worthy investment and at the right time as peripheral banks had to increase retained earnings to rebuild their capital base (Corsetti et al. 2016: 7). Moreover, banks did not have to back sovereign bonds with equity since the BASEL III regulation categorized government debts as safe assets (Fuest, Becker 2017: 88). However, this does not explain why Portuguese banks bought Portuguese bonds, Greek banks bought Greek bonds, and so on, while selling off foreign bonds. Most likely, regulators and governments obliged the banks to hold more sovereign debt since foreign investors were selling these bonds (Acharya 2012). Additionally, banks hoped for a beneficial treatment by the governments if they would succumb to their moral suasion; in fact, a far too optimistic assessment of bank risks was tolerated by the politics (Ongena et al. 2016: 1-2). Unfortunately, this has brought the Southern states into a precarious situation: a stricter banking regulation would imply higher equity requirements for sovereign bonds, but that would overstress the banks and moreover decrease the price of the government bonds. Hence, the diabolic loop hampered a better banking regulation in these countries (Fuest, Becker 2017: 91).

3 Rescue operations and structural reforms: what was done to prevent the break-up of the eurozone?

In the last part, both the proximate and the deeper causes of the euro area crisis were outlined. Thereby, it became evident that immediate countermeasures as well as structural changes were necessary to retain the Monetary Union. In the following, it will be listed what the European decision-makers did in order to find answers to the huge challenges they were confronted with. In general, three main areas can be identified: macroeconomic (rescue) measures, monetary policies and banking regulation. As a matter of course, the countermeasures cannot be examined in detail due to their extent: studying the pros and cons of monetary policy during the crisis, for instance, could easily fill a book on its own. Furthermore, it should be stressed that country-specific efforts to deal with the crisis which happened at the national level cannot be explored. In the case of Greece, for instance, individual aid packages had to be compiled which, inter alia, included debt relieves and private sector involvement in the form of a bail-in (Landeszentrale für politische Bildung Baden-Württemberg 2017a). This part, however, is limited to decisions and actions made on euro area level that affected the Monetary Union as a whole. Yet, finding out which problems were already solved and which shortcomings the Euro's architecture still need to be tackled requires at least a short analysis of the previous rescue steps.

3.1 Macroeconomic (rescue) measures

On macroeconomic level, European politicians had to carry out several interventions to restore stability in the eurozone and to avert the bankruptcy of some of its member states. In order to attain these objectives, they implemented both short-term rescue measures and medium-to-long term structural reforms which encompassed financial support for struggling countries as well as the creation of new and the alteration of existing contracts.

3.1.1 EFSF and ESM

On the 8th of May 2010, the Heads of State and Government of the EU decided to introduce a temporary safety net in order to stabilize the eurozone and to stop speculative attacks on highly indebted member states. Euro countries could borrow from the safety net, but subject to strict conditionality. The safety net was set up for three years, had a maximum volume of €750 billion and consisted of three components (Illing 2017: 70-71): (i) the European Financial Stability

Facility (EFSF) which implied national guarantees with a lending capacity of €440 billion, (ii) European Financial Stability Mechanism (EFSM) which included additional €60 billion, backed by the EU budget and (iii) IMF loans with a volume up to €250 billion. The legal fundament of this package was Article 122 of the Lisbon Treaty[24]. The EFSF was designed as three-year temporary institution which borrowed from the capital markets and could lend to the eurozone countries, while the euro area states guaranteed for the credits (European Stability Mechanism 2017a). Three countries called for EFSF support (Bundesministerium der Finanzen 2017a: 2): Ireland (February 2011; received €17.7 billion), Portugal (June 2011; received €26.0 billion) and Greece (March 2012; received €130.0 billion). Today, the EFSF still exists as a legal entity and issuer of bonds, but it does not grant new loans.

The EFSF, however, was provisional in nature. During the EU summit on the 24th and 25th of March 2011, the Heads of State and Government agreed on the European Stability Mechanism (ESM) which replaced the EFSF and constitutes a permanent mechanism ready for future crisis scenarios (Landeszentrale für politische Bildung Baden-Württemberg 2017b). The ESM was implemented on the 27th of September 2012 and started in October, with a capacity of up to €500 billion. The intension was the same: countries would get cheap loans from the ESM, but had to implement far-reaching economic reforms in order to regain trust of the capital markets. It was hoped that, through the ESM, insolvencies could be prevented and borrowing costs could be reduced (European Stability Mechanism 2017b). The first ESM disbursements with a volume of €41.3 billion were distributed in December 2012 to Spain to recapitalize its banks. In May 2013 Cyprus received financial assistance by the ESM of €6.3 billion and in August 2015 Greece entered a new ESM program with an amount of €86.0 billion (Bundesministerium der Finanzen 2017a: 20). Hence, through the EFSF and the ESM a sum of €254.5 billion was allocated to five countries in total (European Stability Mechanism 2017c).

[24] Art. 122, §2 of the Treaty on the Functioning of the European Union (European Union 2012: 98): *"Where a Member State is in difficulties or is seriously threatened with severe difficulties caused by natural disasters or exceptional occurrences beyond its control, the Council, on a proposal from the Commission, may grant, under certain conditions, Union financial assistance to the Member State concerned."*

3.1.2 European Semester, Reform of the SGP and Fiscal Compact

The European leaders realized that the deficient macroeconomic coordination within the eurozone had to be improved. Accordingly, in 2010 an annual cycle of economic policy coordination was created: the European Semester. In this framework, the European Commission conducts a detailed analysis of EU member states' plans of budgetary, macroeconomic and structural reforms and supplies them with country-specific recommendations for the following 12 to 18 months (European Commission 2016a). Moreover, it monitors the governments' efforts with regard to the objectives of the Europe 2020 strategy[25].

In 2011, the European Semester was flanked by a reform of the SGP which included five regulations and one directive. The so-called "Six Pack" was introduced with the objective of enhanced fiscal surveillance as well as the prevention of macroeconomic imbalances (both excessive deficits and surpluses) and should strengthen the SGP (Bundesministerium der Finanzen 2014). In order to achieve better budgetary policies it was made possible to implement sanctions earlier and more consequently (preventive arm). The Six Pack was closely related to the European Semester as it contained the Macroeconomic Imbalance Procedure (MIP). Within this framework, the European Commission examines a selection of indicators on the basis of a scoreboard and thereby screens the member states for potential imbalances (European Commission 2017b: 6). If the European Commission identifies an excessive imbalance, it provides the respective country with recommendations and monitors the actions taken. The European Commission may also initiate an Excessive Imbalance Procedure (EIP) and force the affect government to submit a plan (Corrective Action Plan) how it intends to bring its indicators back into the accepted range (Fuest, Becker 2017: 159). If a member state continuously fails to comply with the requirements of the EIP, it may face sanctions up to the amount of 0.1% of GDP. Finally, the Six Pack also established a more comprehensive coordination of economic policy (Illing 2017: 82).

The Six Pack was extended in 2013 by the implementation of the "Two Pack", which should increase the budgetary surveillance. The main objective was to have

---

[25] The Europe 2020 strategy was established in 2010 and stipulated key parameters with respect to R&D investments, employment policies, climate change, education and poverty that should be reached until 2020 (European Commission 2017a).

a better conformance of the national budgetary policy procedures of the member states (Bundesministerium der Finanzen 2014). Three uniform budgetary deadlines were determined: (i) Every year, until 30th of April all eurozone member states have to submit their mid-term budgetary plans as well as its growth and employment objectives; (ii) Until the 15th of October, the national budgetary plan has to be submitted at the European Commission. If rejected, they must be revised; and (iii) until 31st of December, every member state has to pass the budget for the next year in its national parliament.

For the purpose of improving cost competitiveness in Europe, the Euro Plus Pact was established in 2011. It should help avoiding large financial and economic imbalances and included measures such as reviews of wage setting arrangements, indexation schemes and public sector wages as well as structural reforms to improve productivity (Gabrisch, Staehr 2014: 4). Deteriorating price and cost competitiveness had been identified as source of economic and financial instability. Hence, policy coordination for competitiveness and convergence should be improved. The Euro Plus Pact was initiated by the German and the French governments and created as intergovernmental agreement between the 19 euro area countries as well as Bulgaria, Denmark, Poland and Romania (European Commission 2015a: 1). It was supposed to complement the European Semester.

In January 2012, it was agreed to establish the "Treaty on Stability, Coordination and Governance in the Economic and Monetary Union", also named "Fiscal Compact". Due to the refusal of the UK and the Czech Republic the treaty was also established as intergovernmental contract, but it was signed by all of the other EU states (Illing 2017: 107-108). A main element of the Fiscal Compact was a mandatory balanced budget rule, implying that the participating countries commit to implementing a fiscal rule which requires them to keep the sovereign budget to be balanced or in surplus into their legislation (European Central Bank 2012a: 101). Moreover, the ESM was linked to the Fiscal Compact[26]. Illing (2017: 108) stresses that it is a crucial point that the German government insisted on

[26] The Treaty (2012: 7) lays down "[...] *that the granting of financial assistance in the framework of new programmes under the European Stability Mechanism will be conditional, as of 1 March 2013, on the ratification of this Treaty by the Contracting Party concerned and, as soon as the transposition period referred to in Article 3(2) of this Treaty has expired, on compliance with the requirements of that Article*".

implementing stricter budgetary rules into the national constitutions since the SGP had already been tightened in 2011 and complemented with the Six Pack. He concludes that this disclosed mistrust towards the European Commission as the reformed SGP left sanction powers to the Commission, while the new Fiscal Compact included automatic mechanisms[27] that were integrated into legislation. Furthermore, a strong focus was put on debt (European Commission 2017b: 3-5): Member states that breach the existing 60% debt-to-GDP ratio can be placed in an Excessive Deficit Procedure (EDP) if they do not sufficiently reduce their debt. Moreover, under the new rules, an increase in public spending must not exceed the medium-term potential GDP growth, unless it is matched by adequate surge in revenues. For the event of a crisis, more flexibility was provided. For example, if there is an unexpected economic downturn, eurozone states with public deficits over 3% of GDP may receive additional time to correct those deficits, subject to the implementation of required structural effort. In order to have a better prevention system, the European Commission and the European Council evaluate the member states' path towards their medium-term budgetary objectives, as specified in their Stability or Convergence Programs presented annually in April. If deemed necessary, a warning, which can be made public, may be addressed to the respective country. The development is then monitored, and if it is not remedied, the European Commission can suggest an interest-bearing deposit of 0.2% of GDP, which has to be approved by the European Council.

3.2 Monetary Policy

By making use of several conventional and unconventional measures, the ECB played a key role in the crisis management. As mentioned before, a detailed analysis of the pros and cons, effects, legal issues and modes of operation cannot be given. However, there should be an overview that outlines the most relevant actions taken in this part and a brief evaluation in section 4.3.

---

[27] The Treaty includes automatic correction mechanisms which should be triggered if the structural deficit limit (or the adjustment path towards it) is violated, which would require euro area countries to set out in national law how and when they would remedy the violation over the course of future budgets. Moreover, for member states in the EDP financial sanctions are triggered earlier and can be gradually increased. If a government fails to reduce the deficit sufficiently, the European Commission can impose fines of 0.2% of GDP. Statistical frauds can be sanctioned with a maximum of 0.5%. In addition, penalties can entail a suspension of EU regional funding (European Commission 2017b: 3-5).

3.2.1 Key interest rates

The key interest rates are a powerful instrument for central banks to steer price levels and economic developments. When the World Financial Crisis hit the eurozone, inflation markedly decreased (see graph 13). The ECB saw its target of price stability at risk and intervened with a low-interest-rate policy[28].

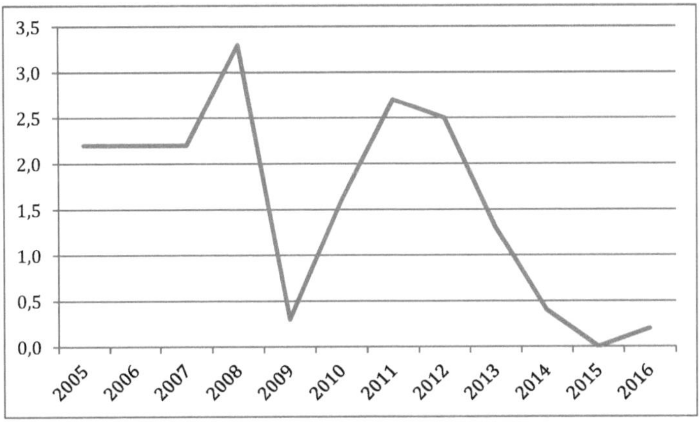

Graph 13: Inflation rate (Annual average rate of change; All-items HICP; Euro area 19)
Source: Eurostat

As shown in graph 14, the ECB significantly lowered its three key interest rates. Euro area banks could therefore easily access fresh capital, which they were supposed to transmit to the real economy. The objective was to ease private sector borrowing conditions and stimulate credit provision to the private sector, thereby enhancing eurozone recovery and returning inflation to the desired levels (European Central Bank 2017b: 45). The interest rate on the deposit facility even

28 It is true that the ECB reacted with lower interest rates to the crisis. However, it should be mentioned that the low-interest-rate policy of the ECB has to be viewed in a broader context. Mersch (2017) points to the fact that has been an economic slowdown in advanced economies (also outside of Europe) not just since the crisis, but for several decades. He highlights that the declining growth rates have been followed by lower long-term interest rates. In fact, there is a large debate on the origins of this development, demographic and technological reasons, for instance, are discussed. Mersch (2017) stresses that, in any case, the natural interest rate, i.e. the real rate of interest in which savings and investments are in equilibrium in an economy operating at its potential, was significantly reduced, necessitating the ECB to bring the market rate below the natural rate. Otherwise, he claims, growth rates would have fallen even further and risk of deflation would have surged tremendously.

became negative in 2014, meaning that banks had to pay for keeping money on their ECB accounts overnight.

However, no central bank can lower the interest rates limitlessly. If a central bank's leeway for supporting measures is already downsized, but further economic shocks occur on the demand side, it has to resort rather to unconventional instruments (Mersch 2016).

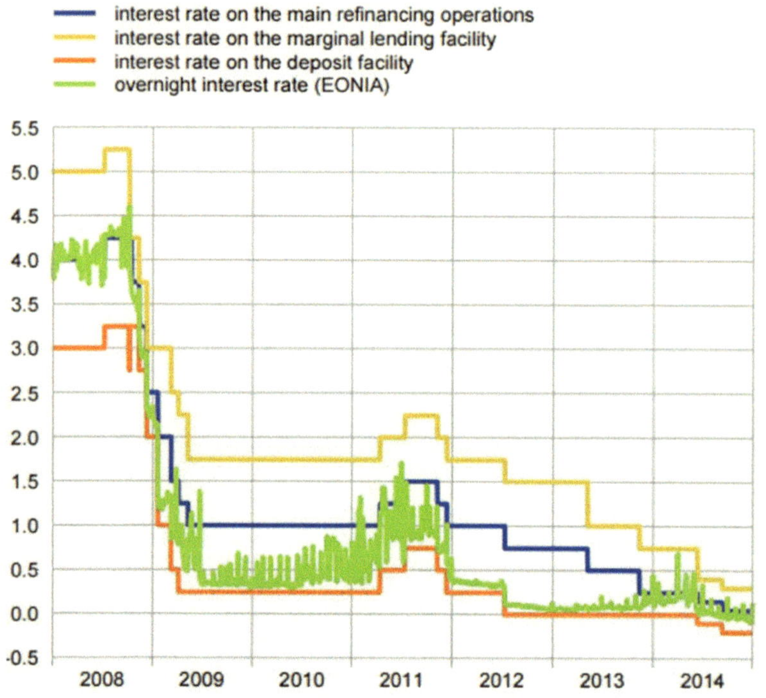

Graph 14: ECB interest rates and the overnight interest rate (percentages per annum)
Source: ECB Annual Report 2014

3.2.2 Unconventional ECB measures

This is exactly what the ECB did in order to approach the loss of confidence in the interbank market, and to increase lending activities, thereby preventing simultaneous illiquidity of several banks. The ECB extended the liquidity provision massively and set up fixed rate tender with full allotment in 2008 (Deutsche Bundesbank 2015: 202). The euro area banks still had to provide collateral for receiving ECB loans, but were steadily less able to do so.

Consequently, the ECB repeatedly lowered the requirements for the collateral such that the banks could access its funds (Deutsche Bundesbank 2015: 205). Moreover, the minimum reserve requirements of 2% were cut by half to 1% (European Central Bank 2016) and the maturity of Longer-Term Refinancing Operations was expanded up to three years (Deutsche Bundesbank 2015: 194).

In addition, the ECB decided to carry out three outright asset purchase programs (APP). In 2010, within the so-called "Securities Markets Program" (SMP) the Euro system bought sovereign bonds of eurozone countries that were particularly affected by the crisis (European Central Bank 2010: 24). The main target was to remedy disruptions on the securities market and to restore a monetary transmission mechanism. Securities of a balance sheet value of €219 billion were purchased under the SMP which was terminated in September 2012.

Despite the ECB's efforts to calm down the capital markets and to relieve crisis-ridden member states, the sovereign debt crisis escalated in 2012. Investors speculated against the Euro assuming that the eurozone would collapse. The decision-makers in the ECB therefore felt compelled to announce a second APP, named Outright Monetary Transactions (OMT) program. In this context, Mario Draghi chose London as location for his famous speech in which he stated that "within our mandate, the ECB is ready to do whatever it takes to preserve the euro. And believe me, it will be enough" (European Central Bank 2012b). Through the OMT program, the ECB was able to carry out a selective purchase of member states' government bonds, which was, however, subject to conditionality: sovereign bonds would only be purchased if the respective country would fulfill its requirements attached to an appropriate EFSF or ESM program (European Central Bank 2012c). The ECB justified this rescue step with the fact that financial fragmentation had created widely divergent borrowing costs for companies and households across the eurozone and again with the malfunctioning of the transmission of monetary policy (Cœuré 2013).

The two purchase programs were flanked by Targeted Longer-Term Refinancing Operations (TLTROs). The extent of these credits depends on the outstanding loan volume of the demanding bank to the non-financial private sector (Bundesbank 2015: 194). A first series of TLTROs was announced in June 2014 and followed by a second series (TLTRO II) as from March 2016. By means of these operations, the ECB intended to stimulate the granting of credits to the private sector and to improve the functional capability of the transmission channel.

As it will become evident below, the OMT program was controversial, but very effective. Nevertheless, the inflation rate kept on following a downward trend (see graph 13). Thus, a deflation risk was identified, but lowering the interest rates in order to restore price stability was not an option due to their already low level. Accordingly, in 2015 the ECB Governing Council opted for a Quantitative Easing (QE) strategy and introduced the Expanded Asset Purchase Program (EAPP) which started as a three-part measure: (i) the third Covered Bond Purchase Program (CBPP3); (ii) the Asset-Backed Securities Purchase Program (ABSPP); and (iii) the Public Sector Purchase Program (PSPP). Originally, the purchases were intended to continue until September 2016, but were prolonged until the end of 2017 in the meantime[29]. The combined monthly purchases amounted to €60 billion on average, but were increased in 2016 to €80 billion (European Central Bank 2017c). Since June 2016, the purchases include both public and private sector securities as the QE was complemented by the Corporate Sector Purchase Program (CSPP). Under this additional program, six national central banks[30] buy bonds of private companies, on the primary as well as on the secondary market (European Central Bank 2017a). The financial sector was excluded from this mechanism. In the course of the crisis, the ECB granted bank credit not only through the standard monetary policy operations, but also through Emergency Liquidity Assistance (ELA). In general, ELA loans are allocated by the national central banks and aim at liquidity provision for banks that are illiquid, but solvent. It is also the national central banks which determine the conditions (such as amount, collateral requirements, interest rate, and so on) and are liable for the risk (Illing, König 2014: 544). Klose (2016: 50) criticizes that there is only few information on ELA credits. He states that Belgium in 2008 and Germany in 2009 made use of ELA credits to stabilize one crisis-stricken bank each. Moreover, he (2017: 51) finds evidence that also in the cases of Ireland and Cyprus ELA loans were provided. The largest ELA credit portfolio, however, can be identified for Greece between 2012 and 2015. Klose presumes that during this period, the Greek Central Bank stepped in whenever Greek sovereign bonds

[29] The Governing Council of the ECB is willing to further extend the program until "*it sees a sustained adjustment in the path of inflation that is consistent with its aim of achieving inflation rates below, but close to, 2% over the medium term*" (European Central Bank 2017c).

[30] The respective national central banks are Banco de España, Banca d'Italia, Banque de France, Deutsche Bundesbank, Nationale Bank van België/Banque Nationale de Belgique, and Suomen Pankki/Finlands Bank (European Central Bank 2017a).

were not accepted for the ECB's refinancing operations. Obviously, Greek banks have been heavily dependent on support through the ELA mechanism (Jones 2015).

3.3 Banking Union

The European leaders understood that the financial sector had to be reformed and to be made safer. Hence, a deeper integration of the European banking system in form of a banking union was pursued. The European Banking Union applies to eurozone member states, but is also open to non-euro area countries. It is based on a Single Rulebook which provides a set of harmonized prudential rules which institutions all over the EU must respect. The Single Rulebook aims at closing regulatory loopholes and should thus contribute to a better functioning of the Single Market (European Banking Authority 2017). It was formed by several initiatives with three of them having key functions: (i) the Capital Requirements Directive IV (CRD IV) which establishes stricter prudential requirements for banks; (ii) the Deposit Guarantee Scheme Directive (DGSD) which enhances protection for depositors and harmonizes the deposit guarantee scheme; and (iii) the Bank Recovery and Resolution Directive (BRRD) which sets up rules for managing failing banks

The Banking Union itself is composed of three pillars. The first is the Single Supervisory Mechanism (SSM) which shifted banking supervision on the European level. Today, the ECB is the central prudential supervisor of financial institutions in the euro area and in those non-eurozone states that joined the Banking Union (European Union 2013). Since November 2014, the ECB supervises the largest banks, while the smaller banks remain under the responsibility of national authorities. The ECB's responsibility includes banks of a certain size, with a major importance to the domestic banking sector or that have been recapitalized by public funds. The ECB and national supervisors work closely together to check for the banks' compliance with the EU banking rules and to approach problems at an early stage (European Commission 2017c). Due to the SSM, the ECB has the power to (i) conduct supervisory reviews, onsite inspections and investigations, (ii) grant or withdraw banking licenses, (iii) evaluate a bank's acquisition and disposal of qualifying holdings, (iv) determine higher capital requirements to counteract current or prevent future financial crises and (v) sanction any breach of EU law on credit institutions, financial holding companies and mixed financial holding companies. Thereby, the ECB is supposed to ensure a

European supervision mechanism that is not prone to the protection of national interests, but should weaken the connection between banks and national finances (European Commission 2015c).

The second pillar is the Single Resolution Mechanism (SRM). It was created to ensure an orderly resolution process of failing banks with minimal costs to taxpayers and to the real economy (European Council 2017). For this purpose, the SRM was complemented by the Single Resolution Fund (SRF) which should end the banks' dependency on support from national budgets. This should also help avoiding situations in which bank resolution at national level would have a major adverse effects on the real economy (European Union 2014: 5). It was planned to build up the SRF over eight years, up to an amount of around €55 billion which is equal to 1% of the amount of covered deposits of all credit institutions authorized in all the banking union participating countries. Moreover, a centralized power of resolution, the Single Resolution Board, was implemented and entrusted with the application of the rules and procedures of the mechanism (European Union 2014: 21). Further objectives of the SRM are the strengthening of confidence in the banking sector, the prevention of bank runs and contagion effects as well as the elimination of fragmentation in the internal market for financial services (European Council 2017).

The third and final pillar of the Banking Union is the European Deposit Insurance Scheme (EDIS), which is not in place yet. EDIS would be built on the current national Deposit Guarantee Schemes (DGSs) which already ensure that deposits up to €100 000 are protected throughout the EU. In the European Commission's (2015b: 3) proposal it is argued that the status quo of national DGSs remains exposed to large regional shocks, which is why EDIS would enhance the resilience of the Banking Union against future crises and increase financial stability. Thereby, according to this view, the level of depositor confidence in a bank would not depend on the bank's location and the extent of domestic interconnection of government and banks. Consequently, the link between banks and their sovereigns would be further reduced. The authors suggest to gradually introduce the common deposit insurance with increasing contributions over time such that, at the final stage, EDIS funds would fully finance the protection of bank deposits (European Commission 2015b: 9-12).

4 Assessment and problems still to be solved

In the previous parts, the origins of the crisis and the countermeasures have been described. Before summarizing and assessing proposals for long-term solutions, however, an intermediate step needs to be taken. The current discussion about which far-reaching reforms of the eurozone's architecture should be implemented reflects the fact that the Currency Union is still not yet placed on a stable foundation. It was protected from a break-up, but there is a consensus that further efforts need to be done to prepare the Euro for future challenges. Accordingly, the rescue measures will be shortly evaluated and additional problems will be portrayed in the following. At the end, it will be identified to which extent the design flaws of the eurozone are rectified and in which areas adjustments are necessary. One aspect should be addressed in advanced, namely that at least most countermeasures have one thing in common: they are controversially discussed and caused large dissent among politicians, economists and other observers. As emphasized before, these debates cannot be elaborated extensively in the present context, but they will be noted.

4.1 Macroeconomic measures

On macroeconomic level both short-run support and long-run structural changes were made. The lack of an institution that provides financial means subject to conditionality to struggling eurozone member states was abolished by establishing the temporary EFSF and the permanent ESM. Before the ESM could be introduced, however, it faced strong opposition in Germany where a legal action against the ESM was taken (Illing 2017: 111). The lawsuit was revised by the German Federal Constitution Court and delayed the inception of the ESM by several months[31]. Riehle (2016: 140-142) criticizes that the ESM was a breach of the no-bail-out clause which, in his opinion, is the most important stability pillar of the Monetary Union. He claims that justifying this step by using Article 122 of the Treaty on the Functioning of the European Union (see section 3.1.1.) is an invalid argumentation since the euro area crisis was not a natural disaster. Illing (2017:72) adds that the EFSF was a step towards mutualization of debt in the eurozone as the EFSF borrowed from capital market investors and was backed by

[31] Finally, the Court approved the ESM, but subject to limiting the German contributions to the mechanism at €190 billion (Bundesverfassungsgericht 2014: 7).

joint guarantees of all Euro states. This thinking was shared by many other economists[32] and led to disputes that eventually brought this issue to justice.

When analyzing the economic appropriateness of EFSF and ESM independently of legal concerns, it is essential to realize once again[33] that differing views on the origins of the crisis exist. As economists disagree on the causes, they consequently have a different understanding of what is necessary to approach the problems. This is reflected in both existing and potential future solutions.

According to the ESM website, the most visible success of both EFSF and ESM is the improved performance of the supported countries: Except for Greece, all member states successfully exited their programs without a follow-up arrangement[34] (European Stability Mechanism 2017c). Hence, the proponents argue that the EFSF and the ESM prevented the disintegration of the euro area and, with regard to the latter, make the Currency Union more stable in the future. When the crisis evolved, it was rather unavoidable to create a safety net as there was no insolvency option or the like. Since the euro area decision-makers decided that no member state should default, there was no genuine alternative (Baldwin et al. 2015: 8). When it comes to a crisis in the future, the ESM as permanent institution can act more rapidly than it was the case in 2010 and is likely to help preventing that a crisis-stricken euro area country experiences an escalating economic downturn. However, the limit of €500 billion could be insufficient if a larger economy, Italy for instance, seeks for financial support. Here, attention should be drawn to the fact that the EFSF and ESM could not calm the capital markets, which was only achieved after the ECB intervened.

It is also deprecated, although from a different perspective, that a eurozone safety net would not be required if the member states would retain an adequate fiscal buffers. By doing so, they were able to apply automatic stabilizers in order to conduct anti-cyclical crisis management (Fuest, Becker 2017: 103-105). As a result, it is suggested to look for and eliminate (institutional) disincentives that led to the lack of fiscal capacity in the run-up to the crisis.

32 See, for example, Fuest and Becker (2017: 61-62).

33 See section 2.2.3.

34 Ireland and Spain in December 2013, Portugal in May 2014 and Cyprus in March 2016.

Closely linked to the ESM is the controversy about the general recovery strategy of overindebted countries. The conditionality attached to the ESM program primarily meant sharp saving obligations and painful structural reforms (European Stability Mechanism 2017b). Generally, an austerity oriented approach was chosen for the eurozone, implying that the member states should save more, spend less and thereby reduce their debt burden. This austerity policy was seen highly critical by many observers. Krugman (2015), for example, accuses European leaders of ignoring the basic macroeconomic knowledge that reducing spending in economies which experience a recession, with no leeway to offset these decreases by lowering interest rates, inevitably worsens the slump. On the opposite side, advocates of austerity policies reply that would be correct to insist on debt reduction since only in this way confidence could be restored and economic recovery be accomplished (Trichet 2010).

At least to some extent, this is a doctrinal question, but some indications suggest that the imposed austerity was too extreme. The IMF, for instance, admits that, in the case of Greece, it used overoptimistic growth assumptions and that a haircut should have been done earlier and in a more drastic way (IMF 2013b). In an ex post evaluation of its program in Greece, it indicates that it has been forced to override its standard rules for providing financial support. Despite having misgivings about Greek sovereign debt sustainability, the IMF agreed on granting monetary assistance, given the danger of contagion (IMF 2013a). Frankel (2015b: 114) claims that it was false to assume that the fiscal austerity strategy would improve the debt-to-GDP ratios: In his view, the fiscal austerity deteriorated the economic situations in Greece and other peripheral states and, as a result, debt-to-GDP ratios rose instead of declining. He (2015a: 432) states that there should have been more focus on competitiveness-enhancing reforms in the rescue strategy of the Troika. Bourgeot (2013: 1) also holds the opinion that the crisis management has clearly not achieved its objective of reducing debt and deficit ratios and blames the austerity policies for economic contradiction and even depression which, in turn, automatically led to an increase in public debt of many member states. Baldwin et al. (2015: 10-11) calculate that the GIPSIC countries accounted for 48% of the fiscal tightening in the euro area even though they form only a third of eurozone GDP. The authors find that this pro-cyclical fiscal tightening worsened the GIPSIC states' economic situations. Moreover, they stress that the effect was aggravated by the fact that, due to time issues, the states mostly decided to increase taxes instead of cutting spending what would have been less contractionary.

De Grauwe (2015: 101-102) considers austerity as inevitable, but criticizes that the reduction of external deficits in crisis states was not compensated by fiscal stimulus in the surplus countries. He deprecates that the deficit countries had to pursue an austerity strategy, but instead of increasing investments the member states with surpluses strived to balance their budgets. Baldwin et al. (2015: 11) add that an active, centralized, aggregated demand management could have mitigated the recession. Corsetti (2015: 90-91) identifies two main reasons for this behavior: on the one hand, the surplus countries feared that any dilution of fiscal and macroeconomic discipline would provoke higher risk premiums for themselves. On the other hand, they did not want to relief the crisis-ridden states from the pressure of implementing painful, but necessary reforms

Especially among German economists, counter-critics can be found. Feld et al. (2016: 2) hold against that the approach to grant further credits in exchanges for reforms was the only way to address the underlying causes of the crisis and moreover succeeded in many respects. According to them, the circumstance that Greece experienced a prolonged crisis can be traced back to the overoptimistic estimations of the Greek economic situation. They hint at observable progress in Ireland, Portugal and Spain and relate the recovering to successful consolidation and structural reforms as well as monetary easing. Fuest and Becker (2017: 107-108) acknowledge that especially in Greece the results of the rescue programs were not successful. However, they point out that the reduction of the public spending was necessary. Furthermore, they draw attention to the fact that not only the demand had been exaggerated before the crisis, but also the economic structure of many member states with a much too expensive administration and an overregulated private sector. The required structural change, however, would need a lot of time and the underlying problems could not be solved by a central decision authority[35] what slowed down progress and deteriorated the recession.

The data reveals that the economic downturns in the crisis-ridden member states indeed worsened after first measures were taken to counteract the euro area crisis. Graph 11 shows that the debt-to-GDP ratios of the GIPSIC countries

35 For Fuest and Becker (2017: 108), rather thousands of small decisions of domestic companies than of a centralized authority form the future model of an economy.

increased after 2010, in particular in Greece[36]. Notably the Irish government achieved a turnaround, but also others managed to come to grips with their debt levels and to break the negative trend. However, looking at the values for 2016 discloses that many member states still struggle with high debt-to-GDP ratios. This applies especially to Greece, Italy and Portugal. However, it is remarkable that no other country out of this selection fulfills 60% obligations. Evidently, the legacy debt constitutes a major problem which still must be tackled.

Similar findings can be drawn from graph 15 which illustrates the growth of GDP since 2010. The GIPSIC countries obviously experienced a recession after 2010. Except for Ireland and Greece, all of them are still below euro area average, but face an upward trend since 2013/14. While the Irish GDP growth is surging, the situation in Greece remains very detrimental.

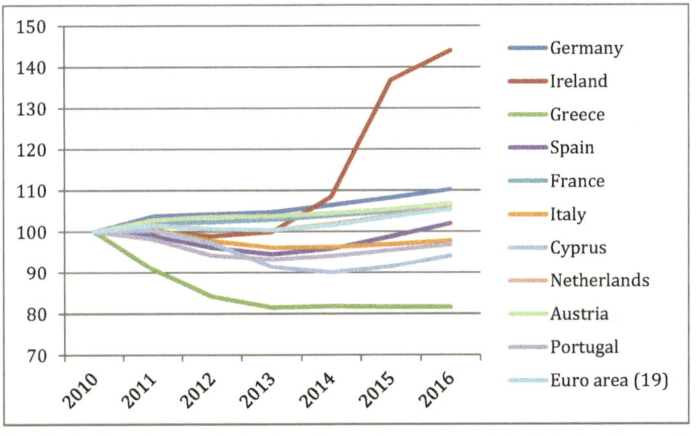

Graph 15: Gross Domestic Product (at market prices; chain linked volumes, index 2010=100)
Source: Eurostat

It is difficult to finally evaluate whether imposing austerity that strictly has been right or wrong. It seems clear that Greece is a special case, which needs to be dissociated from the other members of the Monetary Union. As admitted from official side, mistakes have been made and the adverse effects on the Greek

36 The drop between 2011 and 2012 can most likely be explained with the second rescue package which was that was conceded in 2011 and, among other things, included a debt relieve (see part 3).

economy have been underestimated. For the other countries that went through structural reforms aiming at lowering costs, progress can be found, but of course there is disagreement on whether this is due to or despite the saving efforts. Assessing causality between cuts in spending and economic upswing remains rather indeterminable. Most probably, it would have been helpful for most countries to have more financial scope to counterbalance the effects of cost reduction or to have an external stimulus. Hence, regaining access to the capital markets would have achieved sooner and the economic slump had been less severe, thereby preventing the crisis to become as long-lasting as it did. However, the argument that moral hazard behavior had been present before the crisis and that it could not be excluded that governments had postponed necessary structural reforms not being exposed to great pressure, is valid as well.

In order to minimize scope for moral hazard, the euro area contracts have been reformed and tightened in many areas. Frankel (2015a: 435-436) finds that European leaders aligned their fiscal rules along the lines of the US model as it was believed that the US policies ensure that capital markets do not expect the government to bail out a state, no matter how large the amount of debt may be. However, he detects an error in this reasoning. In his view, the fact that the USA have a fiscal union and let some of their states default on their debts[37], is the crucial factor in this context and not stringency of their rules.

Further criticism is raised by Fuest and Becker (2017: 153-155) who find fault with the implementations of the Six Pack, Two Pack and the Fiscal Compact: As all of these measures contain numerous regulations, procedures and deadlines, they were hard to overview. Moreover, they stress that the formulations were kept very vague; according to their opinion it is not sufficient if rule violations can be sanctioned with toothless instruments such as further warnings and recommendations. Additionally they take a critical look at the flexibility of the fiscal rules: The European Commission is able to acknowledge special circumstances in countries and therefore may accept violations of the debt rules; Fuest and Becker, however, submit that there will always be situations that appear special and necessitate a postponement of a balances budget which is why the

[37] On the one side, Frankel (2015a: 435) refers to 1789 when the US Constitution was ratified and with it the transfer of most spending and taxing powers from the states to the federal level. On the other side, he mentions that eight states had to default on their debts and were not bailed out by the Federal government what constituted a crucial precedent.

strict compliance with the rules would be at least uncertain. This assumption seems reasonable: even though the European Commission (2016b) recognized in 2016 that Spain and Portugal failed to take adequate action to correct their budget deficits, it recommended the European Council to cancel the fines in both cases. In its justification, it inter alia referred to the challenging economic environment in the euro area.

The tightening of the contractual stipulations and the enlargement of the toolkit of the European-level institutions are neither seen exclusively positive. Bofinger (German Council of Economic Experts 2015: 42) notices need for coordinating national budget planning, but considers the design of the European Semester as completely deficient. Indeed, there is evidence that member states did not take great notice of their country-specific recommendations provided by the European Commission (Mussler 2014). Riehle (2016: 39-40) shows little understanding for downward convergence within the MIP framework, meaning that excessive surpluses must be removed as well. He points out that governments have only few instruments to reduce surpluses. Since limiting exports as direct way would not be an option, indirect possibilities to raise export prices had to be chosen, but would weaken the global competitive and export capabilities of the involved state. In his view, such a strategy would only thwart the plan to increase competitiveness in the eurozone. Fuest and Becker (2017: 161) agree on this argumentation and add that the new procedures of the reformed SGP were non-effective. They highlight that, in general, imbalances are not a bad thing, but the result of open economies. In their opinion, the best protection against extreme, harmful imbalances would be well regulated banks and states with responsible budgetary policies. Moreover, they put emphasis on difficulties with the measurement of the relevant indicators and doubt that the eurozone will have enough influence on a member states' aggregated demand. Finally, the GCEE (2015: 31) questions that the new and stricter sanction mechanisms will lead to the desired improvement of fiscal discipline and thereby provide sufficient protection against an uncooperative member country. With regard to the European Semester and the MIP they (2015: 34) state that the high transparency of the scoreboard was beneficial. However, they criticize that the underlying assumption of the MIP was that adverse macroeconomic developments result exclusively from poor policies and could therefore be corrected by introducing better policies. In their Annual Report 2014, they (2014: 218-219) urge that risks were already monitored due to the SGP, the Fiscal Compact and the Banking

Union. Moreover, they raise concerns towards the MIP with respect to the indicative threshold set for excessive imbalances in the current accounts. According to the GCEE there was no consensus on how to set limits for imbalances which is why the experts describe the values of the scoreboard as arbitrary. This would notably hold true for the current account surplus thresholds which were not resulting from a solid scientific and economic analysis. Additionally, they emphasize that the external effects of current account surpluses were controversially discussed among economists who would not agree on the adverse implications of those effects.

Due to the extent of the modifications, the assessment of the reformed SGP, the Fiscal Compact and the European Semester is challenging. Furthermore, it depends on the point of view on the crisis origins. Particularly from Germany criticism arises, even though the Fiscal Compact and the associated obligations to constitutionally implement a debt brake was following pressure from the German government (Illing 2017: 109). Basically, more economic coordination among the member states is preferable and a step in the right direction. The European Semester might not be perfect, but it constitutes a beginning for more transparency and early warning possibilities. The build-up of excessive deficits in a member state should at least be less concealed. The related MIP and the stricter rules and sanctions are well-intentioned and form advancement, but doubts remain with respect to their practical application. Indeed, there is little reason to believe that rule-breaking will not occur in the future, given the flexibility in the interpretation of the rules and the composition of the decision-making bodies[38]. Thus, it is uncertain whether higher fiscal discipline can be expected. Finally, with reference to Spain and Ireland, it could be argued that a tighter regulation and possible resulting fiscal discipline would not guarantee crisis prevention. Having a balanced budget may leave more room for automatic stabilizers, but does not preserve against bubbles in areas such as the real estate sector or other asymmetric shocks that overburden a country.

38 The final decision on potential consequences resulting from the EIP is made by the Council of the European Union (European Commission 2017d). In other words, the Finance Ministers of the EU countries may turn a blind eye on the infringements of others to hope for equal treatment for themselves in case of own rule violations.

4.2 Monetary Policy

As it was explained in part three, the ECB's monetary policy decisions were of vital importance to the euro area. However, the measures taken and their implications were accompanied by great skepticism that even ended up in a legal dispute[39]. Until today, the ECB's actions are contested. Holzhausen and Sikova (2015: 38) examine the effects of the low interest rate policy and find that interest gains could be seen in Spain, Greece and Portugal while German, Belgian and Slovakian households had losses. They conclude that the ECB's zero-rate policy produced and still produces significant redistribution effects within the eurozone through the income channel. They equate these effects with capital transfers from North Europe to the South. Fuest and Becker (2017: 190) identify another disadvantage, namely that the low interest rate policies take pressure off the banks to adjust their portfolios which still require correction efforts. The banking sector, however, also suffers from the low interest rates as it is increasingly difficult to generate sufficient returns with the standard banking business model (Dombret 2017).

The evidence on redistribution effects as well as on further negative repercussions[40] is strong and worth debating, but nevertheless it was plausible and permitted for the ECB to make use of this standard monetary policy instrument. Stiglitz (2017: 15) even alleges that the interest rates should have been lowered earlier in the crisis. He describes that, due to its rigid mandate[41], the ECB could not lower the interest rates as quickly as the FED. Consequently, the Euro appreciated and negatively influenced European economic output. Stiglitz believes that if, by contrast, the ECB had implemented policies to weaken the Euro, it would have stimulated the economies and partially outweighed the effects of the austerity strategy.

The main criticism was directed to the unconventional measures of the ECB. Strong opposition already evolved against the SMP, but in particular the OMT program was and is controversially debated. Especially in Germany, rejection

[39] Claims against the OMT program were submitted in the German Federal Constitutional Court which ruled in favor of the ECB, although with some caveats (Bundesverfassungsgericht 2016).

[40] It should be noted that, for reasons of space, not all adverse and positive effects of the low interest rate policy of the ECB can be mentioned.

[41] Focus on price stability, no growth and employment remits.

against the APPs was observable. It was objected that the ECB was acting outside of its mandate[42] and that the no-bail-out clause was finally offset. The German Council of Economic Experts (2013: 119-122) understand the necessity of the ECB to counteract the belief-driven speculative attacks on the eurozone and acknowledges that its mandate would cover the OMT program in this respect; this, however, would be limited to the extent how unfounded risk premiums for exit risks affect credit conditions in the private sector and interfere with the transmission of monetary policy. Additionally, the GCEE (2013: 119-122) stresses that the clear differentiation between fiscal and monetary policy became blurred since the ECB relinquished a seniority status in the context of the OMT program and thereby took default risks into its balance sheet. This meant that risks were redistributed from the creditors of highly indebted states to the ECB. Furthermore, losses would decrease the profits of the national central banks and thus reduce the revenues of the finance ministers of all Euro states. Hence, they conclude that the mere announcement implied a guarantee of risks through the ECB which the experts consider critical. The President of the Deutsche Bundesbank, Jens Weidmann (Pennekamp, Schäfers 2013), shares this view and deduces that the price stability is threatened if the dividing lines between fiscal and monetary policy become blurred. Moreover, he sees the independency of the ECB at risk.

For Fuest and Becker (2017: 61-62), the ECB's decision to carry out the APPs brought about a paradigm shift since the purchases of sovereign bonds abolished the no-bail-out clause and the public financing prohibition. They (2017: 96) admit that the OMT program was able to calm down investors, but point to the fact that, from then on, the consequences of a state bankruptcy were imposed on the taxpayers of all member states and the incentives of fiscal discipline were further diluted. Sinn (2014: 29) highlights that the Monetary Union is heading for joint liability among the member states due to the APPs. In his opinion, these far-reaching steps will not lead to the establishment of a federal state in the real sense of the word[43], but to a unitary state that will be created through a disregard of the population's preferences and through the actions enforced by a

[42] Notably with respect to Article 123 of the Treaty on the Functioning of the European Union.

[43] Sinn (2014: 29) defines a federal state as "*a union of equals who by their own will, decide to come together and provide mutual assistance*".

technocratic institution that acts completely independently and that pre-determines parliaments' subsequent decisions.

It may well be that some German economists or other observers exaggerate in some points, but there is much to suggest that their concerns are well-founded. The effectiveness of the OMT program, however, is indisputable. As it becomes visible in graph 10, the borrowing costs for the crisis-ridden member states dropped sharply after 2012, accompanied by an analogous decline in the euro area interest rate spreads.

Frankel (2015a: 436) emphasizes that the mere announcement was so successful that the OMT program never had to be practically implemented. Bofinger (German Council of Economic Experts 2015: 39) adds that the eurozone most likely had broken apart if the ECB had not been prepared to intervene forcefully on financial markets by means of the OMT[44]. Saka et al. (2014: 27) even go so far as to say that the OMT mechanism should be formalized into European law. They put focus on the specific insolvency risk and consider the ECB's decision as crucial step for abolishing this fragility. According to them, unnecessary contagion, that is, contagion that does not include fundamentals, was curbed by the ECB which is why it would not be smart to end the program.

Finally, the issuance of ELA credits through the national central banks should be examined. The lack of transparency was described in section 3.2.2., but there are more negative aspects. Naturally, there is nothing to be said against helping an illiquid, but solvent bank. However, Illing and König (2014: 544-545) find several counterarguments: first of all, through its marginal lending facility, the ECB is providing unlimited overnight liquidity against qualified collateral anyway. Hence, a bank would only demand ELA loans if it has exhausted its pool of adequate collateral. In this case, however, a bank is highly likely to have a solvency problem which is why further financial means through ELA could delay the filing of insolvency. Furthermore, the authors explain that it would be more difficult to prove illegal monetary public financing in this context, which, of course, is also prohibited for the usage of ELA credits. They conclude that the ELA procedures

[44] Bofinger's colleagues agree that the OMT announcement was very expedient, but add for consideration that the improved refinancing conditions for the member states might have decreased pressure on the political decision-makers to promptly implement consolidation measures and structural reforms (German Council of Economic Experts 2013: 120-121).

should be reorganized: on the one side, there should be more transparency and on the other side, the ECB should monitor the allocation of ELA loans.

Considering the pros and cons, it can be stated that most of the ECB's unconventional methods were at least in a regulatory grey area, but the correct choice since there was no alternative rescue framework. Some of the critics also arrive at this conclusion, but criticize the resulting postponement of structural reforms (Fuest, Becker 2017: 75). In any case, the ECB should be released from feeling obliged to intervene against self-fulfilling speculative attacks that originate from the specific insolvency risk of the Euro countries. Otherwise, its independency will be eliminated definitively and the differentiation between fiscal and monetary policy will removed. De Grauwe (2015: 105) reinforces this finding by questioning the future effectiveness of the OMT program by asserting that the strong German opposition significantly impaired the program's credibility. Ultimately, the guidelines for the ELA practice should be reformed.

4.3 Banking Union

The need for a centralized banking supervision and resolution was recognized by the European leaders. Consequently, they established the three-pillar Banking Union of which two thirds were already implemented[45]. The general perception is that this step was both vital and well realized. Corsetti (2015: 88), for instance, believes that the future of the Currency Union depends on establishing an institutional framework that credibly delivers stability at eurozone level and appreciates that significant progress has been made with the Banking Union. Baldwin et al. (2015: 3) put the Banking Union in context with the famous Draghi speech of 2012 and argue that these two measures were essential for rescuing the euro area. They (2015: 11-12) highlight that the demonstrated political will and the rapid progress on establishing a functioning Banking Union was of great importance since it helped abolishing fears of the diabolic loop pulling more countries into even more severe problems.

However, some economists identify some shortcomings in the framework of the Banking Union and point out that further modifications are required. Feld et al. (2016: 3) see need for a European banking or even integrated financial supervisor

[45] It should be noted that the third pillar of the Banking Union, the European Deposit Insurance Scheme, will be treated as proposal in part five and therefore does not appear in section 4.3.

which would be institutionally independent from the ECB and which would be responsible for both micro- and macroprudential supervision. In fact, it is frequently discussed whether the ECB should be responsible for the banking supervision. Riehle (2016: 232), for example, demonstrates that there might be a contradiction if the ECB demands more bank lending to companies, but is simultaneously in charge of monitoring and limiting the credit risk of banks.

Criticism is also formulated with regard to the SRM and its SRF. The GCEE (2015: 27) questions the effectiveness of the SRM and demands further competences for the resolution authority such that it can also initiate and implement resolutions for smaller banks. Moreover, they continue, discretionary leeway for creditor participation should be eliminated and exceptions only possible in the event of a systemic crisis after high institutional hurdles are overcome. Corsetti (2016: 20) criticizes that the SRF is small relative to the size of the banking sector and stresses that strict execution of the resolution rules (bail in) would seem problematic in some countries[46]. Riehle (2016: 232) endorses the communitization of bank risks and the mandatory bank submissions for the SRF. Nevertheless, he (2016: 234-236) finds some counterpoints: In his view, for global players such as the Deutsche Bank, it would be justifiable to co-finance a restructuring or an insolvency of Spanish or Italian Banks. However, for banks such as the German Sparkassen, which have mainly national businesses with manageable risks, it would be unfair to pay for risks that arise in markets in which they do not operate. Furthermore, he indicates that the largest credit risks were located in the Southern Europe banking systems, implying that the largest losses were likely to accrue there. Due to the gradual sharing of bank risks, he fears that German banks will become liable for former and not only future liabilities of banks of other eurozone member states.

Apart from these objections, Corsetti et al. (2016: 20-21) state that the Banking Union did not solve the diabolic loop. They see remarkable, but insufficient progress in this respect and back this assumption with data showing that many

[46] There is strong evidence for this proposition (Kirchgaessner 2016, Mussler 2016): In 2016, the Italian bank Monte dei Paschi di Siena was heading for bankruptcy. The new rules under the BRRD stipulate a bail-in of shareholders, which in case of Monte dei Paschi included many small investors. The Italian government of the former Prime Minister Matteo Renzi, however, did not want to displease voters due to a crucial referendum in December 2016. As a result, the Italian government attempted to circumvent or at least postpone the bail-in and finally succeeded.

eurozone countries (exceptions are, for instance, Ireland and the Netherlands) still have a government debt portfolio strongly biased towards domestic debt holdings. According to their data, notably in Spain, Italy and Portugal the home bias problem is still at a critical level and cannot be overcome by the Banking Union alone.

Another issue is that, following the argumentation of Baldwin et al. (2015: 9), the banking sector is still in a weak condition due to poor crisis management and the absence of a recapitalization. They argue that it should have been a priority to cut bank leverage and to recapitalize banks, ideally with the help of foreign investors or EU institutions in order to prevent the concentration of risk within individual countries. Baldwin et al. compare the eurozone with the USA where the risks were concentrated on the public balance sheet and quarrel with the fact that the rules of the Monetary Union prohibited to do likewise[47].

Based on this short analysis, some conclusions should be drawn. In principle, the Banking Union was an essential reform for the Monetary Union. Its relevance arises not only from its stabilizing function for the banking sector, but also from the demonstrated ability of the EU to quickly implement a major structural change in order to react to an enormous challenge. For the eurozone it is vital to have this Banking Union, even if the above mentioned shortcomings are valid and require rethinking and improvements in some areas. It is equally important to be aware of what the Banking Union can achieve and which problems necessitate further efforts.

4.4 Competitiveness levels

Section 4.1. showed that the macroeconomic measures averted the collapse of the Currency Union and potentially heaved it on a more stable fundament. However, it also became evident that the high debt levels, for example, could not yet be lowered adequately. Concerning the competitiveness levels, it should again be emphasized, that it is insufficient to evaluate a country's competitiveness on the basis of a few aggregated, macroeconomic parameters. Still, they give an

[47] It should be mentioned that there are sound reasons for these rules as Jeroen Dijsselbloem , President of the Eurogroup, pointed out: "*There have always been and will always be bankers who say: 'We need more public money to recapitalize our banks' and I will resist that very strongly because it is, again and again, hitting the taxpayer*" (Kirchgaessner 2016).

impression on how the eurozone developed after the outburst of the crisis and on the current status

The real unit labor costs were drastically lowered in Ireland as well as Portugal and also in Spain they are on a relatively low level, as it can be seen in graph 16. In Greece, Cyprus and Italy reduction is observable, but their values remain significantly higher than in other member states[48].

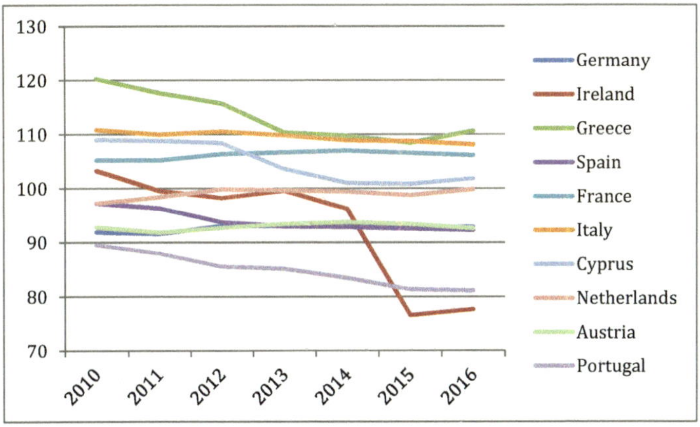

Graph 16: Real Unit Labor Costs (1999=100)
Source: Ameco, own calculations

In graph 17 it becomes evident that the rescue measures took great effect on the inflation rates. Unlike in the decade before the crisis, Germany was markedly above euro area average in the period between 2010 and 2016. Same holds true for Austria. In Portugal, Ireland and Italy, numbers slightly below average can be identified, while the rate of price increases was close to zero in Spain and Cyprus. In Greece even deflation is noticeable.

[48] No new index (e.g. 2010 = 100) is used to compare current levels with pre-crisis conditions.

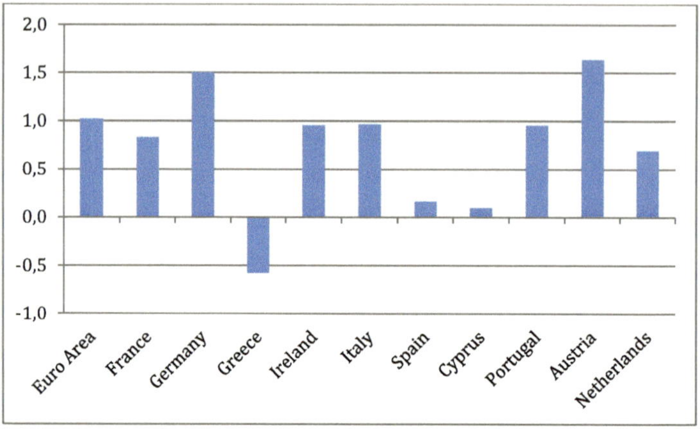

Graph 17: Average inflation rates (GDP deflator), 2010-2016
Source: IMF International Financial Statistics, own calculations

Naturally, lower prices in the South and higher prices in the North can make an impact on the trade imbalances. In fact, graph 18 illustrates that most countries considerably improved their current account to GDP ratio, which is especially true for Greece where the simultaneous recession was most rigorous, but also for Portugal and Cyprus (see graph 15). Moreover, it is worth noting that Germany has a large surplus despite the higher inflation rates. However, it is difficult to infer arguments from this data.

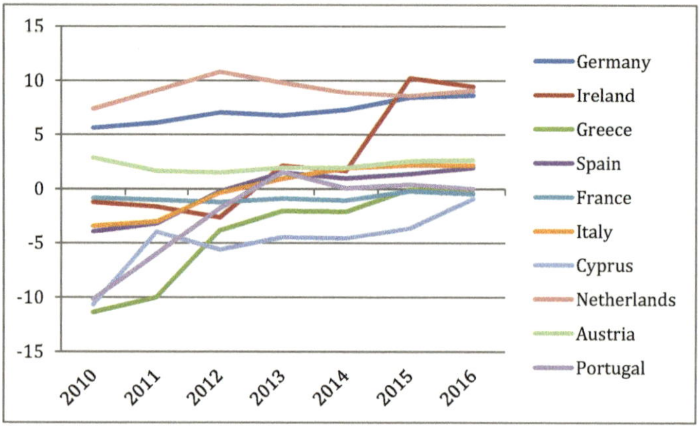

Graph 18: Current Account Balance (in % of GDP)
Source: IMF, WEO database

Graph 18 does not reveal to which extent the changes are caused by higher exports or lower imports. In the case of Greece, for example, it seems reasonable to assume that the drastic saving efforts led to lower imports and thereby became key driver for a better current account balance.

The real labor productivity (Graph 19) developed less volatile than before the crisis. Generally, neither large increases nor sharp drops occurred in the years between 2010 and 2016, with Ireland being the exception. The negative trend in Italy has continued and leaves the country in a relatively weak position in this respect.

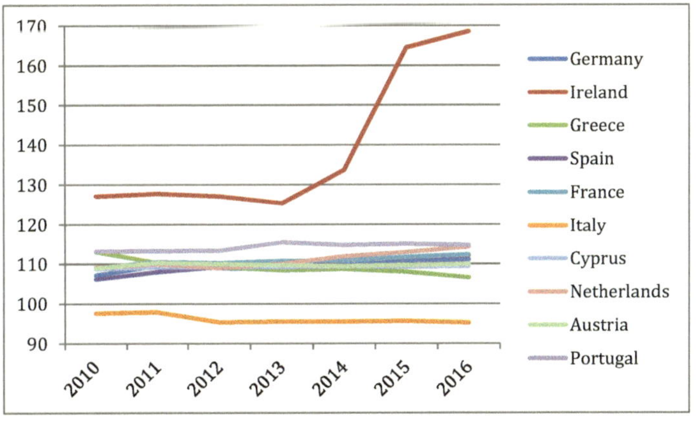

Graph 19: Real Labor Productivity (per person, 1999=100)
Source: Eurostat, own calculations

With regard to the total R&D expenditure in percentage of GDP (Graph 20) it can be stated that few things have changed. While Germany, France, Austria and the Netherlands kept investing above or close to euro area average, the GIPSIC countries used below-average financial means. The increasing numbers for Greece should be seen in consideration of its negative GDP growth.

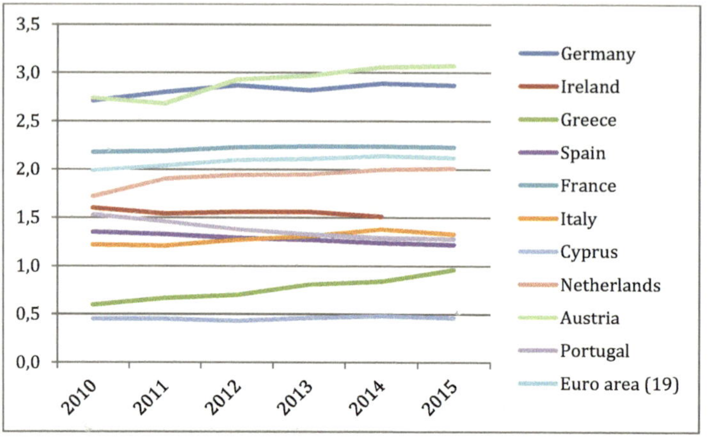

Graph 20: Total R&D Expenditure (in % of GDP)
Source: Eurostat

The comprehensive countermeasures to fight the crisis are reflected in the evolution of the parameters used to show the divergence process before the crisis. In some areas, real progress is obvious, but concurrently large differences remain. While Germany has rather constant growth rates and a well-functioning economy, Greece in particular, but also Italy and Portugal lag behind in several categories and seem to have severe structural problems that adversely affect their competitiveness and economic performance. A very positive example is Ireland, which managed to clearly improve its conditions. In general, the large divergence in price competitiveness seems to be shrinking, but there are justifiable doubts whether this will lead to an equal basis anytime soon. This perception is reinforced by several research publications[49]: The GCEE (2016: 76-80) is surprised about the prolonged economic output gap in the Monetary Union and mentions the high private debt level as well as misallocation of production factors as major sources, but also points to France and Italy where – unlike in other member states – the price competitiveness had not been improved significantly since 2008. For the other Euro countries, they urge that the reversal of the current account balances and the reduction of unit labor costs alone do not form a satisfactory proof for the correction of macroeconomic adverse developments.

49 See also: The European Commission (2016c: 8-18) identifies need for further convergence to create more resilience and equal terms in the euro area.

The experts admit that the positive current account developments could be traced back to an increase of exports, but admonish that in some states the export levels had not sufficiently grown and that the imports were not structurally decreased, but only analogously to the contraction of GDP. Consequently, the GCEE fears that the current account balances of these Currency Union members will again turn negative in the future. With regard to the unit labor costs, the economists present results of an in-depth analysis: Among other things, they state that a large part of the nominal unit labor cost reduction had been achieved through falls in employment and not through actual wage cuts. Moreover, they criticize the lack of a necessary reallocation from non-tradables producing sectors to tradables producing sectors and see this deficient allocation reflected in the labor productivity. Hence, they conclude that the previous adjustment processes could not be deemed successful. The IMF (2016: 5) adds that the reform impetus in the Currency Union is diminishing, even though sizeable imbalances at the national level would require further structural efforts.

4.5 Further obstacles and problems

It can already be anticipated that the eurozone decision-makers are (still) facing a large-scale economic challenge. However, there are additional issues that are discussed in the literature and will be briefly mentioned in this section[50]. Major doubts about a successful adjustment process in the euro area arise from cultural differences. Riehle (2016: 296-298) states that there were large social and especially economical cultural differences between the Euro states that seem insurmountable when it comes to reforming the Currency Union. He divides the eurozone into North and South and describes fundamental differences in social, economic and systemically structures: in his view, the Greek citizens, for instance, had a completely different thinking about the role of the state and the functioning of an administration. His argumentation is not empty handed: in fact, the taxation system in Greece does not have much in common with the German or French one[51]. Not only for the special case Greece, but also for Italy and France many

50 It is not claimed that every single problem or hurdle that may exist is reviewed in the following, but rather a selection of topics deemed most relevant.

51 Mitsopoulos and Pelagidis (2011: 119) find that "[...] *in Greece a disproportionally large percentage of personal income tax returns declare incomes low enough so as to ensure that about half the households that file tax returns essentially do not pay any income tax*".

characteristics can be found that distinguish them from Germany, Austria, Finland or the Netherlands. With respect to Italy, Riehle (2016: 300-302) argues that it had social structures that inhibit competitive convergence and resemble Greece. In his opinion (2016: 308-314), France rejected an ordoliberal economic system and preferred a system in which the state frequently intervenes into the economy and neglects the advantages of a market economy with high competition. For Riehle it is clear that France and also Southern member states strived for establishing this understanding on European level, which translates into common liability and shared risks levering the market economy principles.

In general, it seems reasonable to argue that the euro area contains heterogeneous countries that differ in their preferences of how to design an economic and political system. Moreover, it is obvious that these differences contributed to conflicts in the past and still do today. Hence, posing the question whether the Euro states united within a currency framework which does not function due to economic, but also cultural differences is a legitimate objection. However, concluding that an orderly break-up of the euro area would be the best choice, as Riehle does, is open to question as well.

Fuest and Becker (2017: 18-19), for example, counter that every European country has highly efficient world class companies that exist along with dysfunctional, inefficient structures being prone to corruption and mismanagement. In their view, it is not the national character, but institutions that are responsible for misalignments and the results of collective actions. They (2017: 114-116) also identify a crucial conflict between France and Germany: according to them, the low inflation rate policy of the Maastricht-Treaty as well as the fiscal rules of the SGP comply with the German requirements, but cause tensions in France as high wage agreements cannot be compensated with inflation and thus lead to higher unemployment. This would be perceived as compulsion in France and consequently provoked resentments. After all, they do not consider these disputes as insurmountable, which seems more prudent than being in favor of the elimination of the Monetary Union.

Nonetheless, both authors (2017: 71-72) point to another, related issue by stating that the rescue operations left an enormous political damage what especially counted for Greece where the rescue measures were characterized as a dictation from Berlin and Brussels. Fuest and Becker describe that during the crisis there were recurring patterns: the Greek governments agreed on saving measures, the Greek population protested against that, the Greek government refused the implementation and finally the Troika enforced it. Furthermore, they (2017: 72-73) refer to Ireland which was forced to rescue its banks which had high debt towards German and French banks[52]. Moreover, in Cyprus there was a bail-in which not only affected major investors but also small savers. Zenios (2016: 603) indicates that this was unique in the eurozone (as small savers were protected elsewhere) and detects that the bail-in violated several principles for a fair restructuring of bank liabilities, which would explain the Cypriot population being upset about this process.

In conclusion[53], it cannot be denied that in the recent years the solution finding and enforcement operations have left the eurozone scarred. National resentments arose, were fueled by leading politicians[54] and hamper a constructive cooperation. However, it is also true that despite these political rifts major reforms such as the Banking Union could be implemented. Additionally, the latest elections in Europe, in particular in Austria and France[55], demonstrated that a pro-Euro mentality can still convince majorities.

4.6 Interim Conclusion

In the euro area, a clear upwards trend is observable: GDP is growing (see graph 15), private investments are rising and the forecasts are positive (European Central Bank 2017d: 1). This is good news, but should not disguise the fact that the Monetary Union is still far from being on settled on a solid, well-functioning

---

52 Further evidence on this claim was given by Kevin Cardiff, former secretary general of the Irish department of finance, who testified to a Dublin inquiry into the causes of the crisis that the Irish government was "*pushed quite hard*" by the Troika (BBC 2015).

53 Another issue was raised by Sinn who called attention to the TARGET2 balances which exhibited large imbalances. In fact, the claims of the German Bundesbank largely increased and still amounted to more than €850 billion on 31st of May 2017 (Deutsche Bundesbank 2017). Certainly, the TARGET2 balances should to be strictly observed. However, they would only translate into real costs if a member state would leave the Monetary Union and will therefore not be further elaborated.

54 For instance: Jannis Varoufakis calling Wolfgang Schäuble an "*incompetent little man*" (Welt 2016), Matteo Renzi stating that the German austerity strategy would destroy Europe and favor exclusively Germany (Zschäpitz 2016) or Horst Seehofer labeling the Greek policies as "*circus*" (FAZ 2015).

55 In Austria, Alexander Van der Bellen was elected Federal President; in France, Emmanuel Macron won the Presidency over Marie le Pen and now even has an absolute majority in the French parliament. Both politicians had pursued electoral campaigns characterized by pro-European and pro-eurozone contents.

fundament. The short-run prospects may be fine, but the preceding analysis has shown that the measures which led to this sound development are controversial and not necessarily suitable for the future. Moreover, the underlying design flaws of the eurozone are not remedied sufficiently. The following points are considered to be open issues that require further adjustments: (i) The diabolic loop is still existent; (ii) the legacy debt is overwhelmingly high and prevents recovery as well as reform steps; (iii) fiscal moral hazard remained and is not ruled out in the future due to low credibility of the fiscal rules; (iv) the vulnerability of member states towards self-fulfilling vicious circles (specific insolvency risk) was not eliminated; (v) the ECB's conventional and unconventional measures include adverse legal and economic aspects, which is why solutions should be found to release the ECB from its crisis policy; (vi) excessive imbalances in external balances are not sufficiently downsized in some member states and may reappear in others; (vii) relating thereto, the economic performance and competitiveness levels within the Currency Union continue to differ, leaving heterogeneous countries exposed to homogeneous monetary policy and asymmetric shocks.

5 Proposals

In the literature, a great number of proposals that attend to long run adjustments of the eurozone's architecture can be found. As mentioned in the introduction of this thesis, not all of them can be presented, but a selection of those considered most relevant[56] will be given. Besides, it should be outlined how long run is understood in the present context: Long-run solutions mean measures that solve the identified underlying shortcomings and thereby base the euro area on an intact foundation. In a broader sense, all proposals that deal with the analyzed design flaws and aim at making the Monetary Union run smoothly and become robust against future crises as well as asymmetric shocks can be included. Since it is uncertain whether the next crisis will occur in three, five, twenty or fifty years, it does not make sense to determine a concrete time frame. Thus, ideas that solve a key problem immediately as well as in ten years or even later can be taken into account. The decisive factor is that a solution must permanently remedy one or more of the construction errors and not only fight symptoms with a flash in the pan character[57].

In order to get a better overview, the proposals are divided into two main categories. On the one side, it is called for further integration steps in the euro area. Naturally, the degree of integration as well as the design varies from suggestion to suggestion. In any case, these calls are in line with the original understanding that a crisis would unfold the need for more integration and impose the required pressure on the member states to do so. On the other side, it is demanded to ensure that the eurozone governments have more individual responsibility, that is, considerable freedom with regard to their national budget planning, but also strong accountability. Supporters of this view often demand that control and liability must not diverge, implying that consequences of irresponsible activities should be exclusively borne by the originators. They doubt that deeper integration is feasible, at least not without inducing one-way permanent transfers.

56 Some outdated or imprecise proposals are not taken into account. Moreover, some ideas overlap and thereby allow for choosing only one suggestion out of several.

57 For example, the EFSF was of temporary nature, created with the objective to help member states with liquidity problems on short notice. Its successor, on the contrary, was permanently established and, given it is not removed, can theoretically persist for an indefinite period.

Finally, it needs to be clarified which criteria are used to evaluate the proposals. The final assessment will be carried out in the next part, but it seems reasonable to attach criticism and counterarguments directly to the explanations. Accordingly, it should be highlighted that propositions for reforms can be reviewed with respect to their political and economic feasibility which will be done in the present context. However, the decision how to change the EMU has also a normative dimension: how do the European people *want* their Currency Union to be like? Some ideas may be irrational from an economic perspective, but serve a purpose of social character or the like. This normative viewpoint will not be incorporated in the upcoming analysis.

5.1 Proposals including more integration in the eurozone

5.1.1 Completing the Banking Union

European Deposit Insurance Scheme

EDIS was already presented as third pillar of the Banking Union which is not yet effective and therefore treated as proposal for future adjustments. In its recently published reflection paper the European Commission (2017e: 19-20) describes the EDIS as outstanding key component of the Banking Union which was crucial to mitigate the diabolic loop. It argues that EDIS would thus provide a stronger and more uniform insurance cover for all small depositors in countries participating in the Banking Union. In fact, asymmetric shocks would not have regional impacts, but could be absorbed by the scheme. Increased financial stability would then have positive repercussions on the whole eurozone.

There are alternative options to the European Commission's concept of wholly mutualization of the existing deposit insurance funds. The Council of the European Union thinks of a common guarantee scheme which includes mandatory lending between national deposit guarantee schemes in case of need (German Council of Economic Experts 2016: 273). If the loans were fully repaid, the degree of mutualization would be lower than under the standard EDIS. Gros (2013: 1) proposes that current DGSs should remain national, but that a European Reinsurance Fund should be established to reinsure risks that are too large to be covered individually. In his model, minimal standards for the national DGSs would be set by an EU directive, premiums paid by the national DGSs would finance the fund and reinsurance would only be used for large losses. Thereby, he argues, in case of large shocks the depositor confidence would still be strong, while national authorities were provided with appropriate incentives. With regard to the latter point, he (2013: 5-6) endorses differences in the risk premiums to be paid according to different levels of risks, even though the determination of appropriate risk premiums would be difficult. Moreover, in the event of a systemic shock to a large member state, the ESM had to jump in. Eventually, he focuses on the legacy problems of the banking sector and recommends that the mechanism should be introduced stepwise to ensure that it does not distribute, ex post, the legacy debt from the present crisis

The GCEE (2016: 272-274) discusses the proposals and finds several advantages arising from sharing compensation risks, among them diversification benefits, higher financial stability, convergence of deposit rates, loosening the ties between governments and banks by being able to cope with banking crises that purely national guarantee schemes could not bear and thus would necessitate governmental intervention. However, they urge that a common deposit insurance, if not designed correctly, could set incentives for member states to shift risks to European level which would violate the principle of unity of liability and control. Furthermore, they argue that it should not be implemented without making explicit agreements on fiscal backstops since a systemic crisis, straining the common scheme itself, could provoke uncertainty whether the guarantees are credible and bank runs may follow. Consequently, they criticize that such a fiscal backstop was not integrated into the proposal of the Council of the European Union. Ultimately, they list several prerequisites they consider necessary: (i) As member states could potentially be adversely incentivized by the common bank-financed guarantee fund, some measures should be implemented to avoid undesired behavior. For instance, parts of the compensation costs could be borne exclusively by banks of the country in which the affected bank is located; (ii) current risks should be removed from banks' balance sheets before introducing the scheme; (iii) the other two pillars of the Banking Union had to be effective and finalized; (iv) the diabolic loop had to be mitigated by removing privileges of sovereign exposures; and (v) more harmonization in the banking system, for instance with regard to insolvency and foreclosure law, would be helpful.

Fuest and Becker (2017: 167-170) acknowledge that deposit guarantees generally have an important stabilization functioning in the banking sector and state that the crisis had shown that small countries with a large banking sector have difficulties with the redemption of the guarantee. Nonetheless, they disapprove of introducing an obligatory common deposit insurance mechanism.

They explain that less robust banks would benefit, as the difference between a solid and a weak bank would get offset for savers who would normally always prefer a bank with a high equity ratio. Moreover, they stress that banks as private companies had vested interest in proving their clients that the deposits are save. In conclusion, a cross-border diversification was in the interest of the insurance institutions anyway and had not to be enforced by law. Finally, both economists see the possibility of regulation shopping since location competition with lax regulations for banks would arise due to the shared costs[58].

Fiscal backstop for the Single Resolution Fund

Another target of the European Commission for completing the Banking Union is the implementation of a fiscal backstop for the SRF. Thereby, it reacts to the point of criticism that severe problems could necessitate financial support exceeding the means available in the fund. The European Commission (2017e: 20) suggests using the ESM as fiscal backstop, knowing that some decision-making procedures and technical provisions of the ESM had to be streamlined such that the backstop could be activated in a swift manner and provide high level cost efficiency for the SRF. Alternatively, loans or guarantees could be granted by the member states. In the Commission's opinion, this approach would respect national prerogatives, but was rather ineffective: For instance, difficulties in mobilizing the committed funds could occur in the event of a crisis, making it potentially useless when most needed.

Allard et al. (2013: 21-22) also deem necessary to establish a fiscal backstop for the Banking Union to be prepared for systemic crises that may overburden the private sector contributions. They argue that the mere existence of a common backstop would help anchor confidence in the banking system of the Monetary Union. However, they believe that the ESM can only provide a bridge to such permanent fiscal backstops and demand a credit line from pooled fiscal resources which could provide better insurance against financial risks.

58 Fuest and Becker argue that large banking sectors are beneficial for small countries as they yield tax incomes. However, if costs are shared among the member states in case of bank failure, incentives for a strict banking regulation may be lowered.

5.1.2 Macroeconomic Stabilizers

The analysis prior to this part showed that there is a lack of macroeconomic stabilizers on euro area level. Especially those who put emphasize on the specific insolvency risk and the member states' dependency on sometimes irrationally behaving capital markets demand for stabilization functions. In this regard, several options are debated in the literature.

European Unemployment Benefit Scheme

A European Unemployment Benefit Scheme (EUBS) is one of these options. The European Commission (2017e: 26) also lists this possibility in its reflection paper and envisages a reinsurance fund for national unemployment schemes which would provide more leeway for national public finances and help to escape from a crisis faster and stronger. Beblavý et al. (2015: 11-14) submit precise thoughts on the rationale and challenges ahead. They identify major advantages of an EUBS stemming from its anti-cyclical, automatic and rapid character, the fact that those who suffer most from a recession would be the ones who would benefit and the associated type of expenditure which would have a high multiplier effect since households could sustain their consumption levels. Furthermore, four finance possibilities would come into question: a payroll tax, a corporate tax, contributions of member states according to GDP and the issuance of common debt. The authors are prone to the third variant.

In accordance with the European Commission, they refer to a range of obstacles which concern the political feasibility and the practical implementation. At first, Beblavý et al. take note of differences of the existing national unemployment benefit schemes (UBSs): as they reflect national preferences, they differ in particular with respect to eligibility requirements, generosity of the benefits and the duration. Consequently, this implies that a common system would presuppose wide-ranging harmonization efforts. However, Beblavý et al. believe that large-scale reforms could be circumvented by earmarking the financial support which is transferred within the Monetary Union for unemployment benefits since the governments could thereby distribute the financial aid according to their national legislations. On the downside, governments could be incentivized to increase their benefits with the EUBS bearing the costs. Thus, the authors also review implementing a genuine EUBS through which the financial transfers would be steered directly to the unemployed individuals. They admit that this would require more harmonization, but from their point of view this drawback could be limited by offering workers to choose between a national and a European labor contract that only differs in terms of the unemployment insurance scheme.

Regardless of these arguments, the GCEE (2015: 33-34) neglects the need for an EUBS. From the experts' point of view, creating a pan-European unemployment insurance is very difficult to realize due to the just mentioned design differences. They also urge that backing up unemployment with a European system would probably be accompanied by significant incentive problems. Thirdly, they expect that an EUBS would lead to redistribution effects since the origins of unemployment are not only cyclical but also structural. Thus, permanent transfers were likely to result. Allard et al. (2013: 20) share this perspective and therefore add that, given the large differences in long-term unemployment levels across the eurozone, the focus should be limited to short-term unemployment benefits, which would be closely linked to negative shocks. This would different for long-term unemployment which would be more directly connected to labor market and other structural rigidities. Otherwise, permanent transfers from low-unemployment level regions to high-unemployment regions would immediately emerge. However, they explain that focusing on short-term unemployment protection would diminish the extent of smoothing.

European Investment Protection Scheme

An alternative to the EUBS would a European Investment Protection Scheme (EIPS) which would safeguard investment when a recession hits a member states. In this proposal by the European Commission (2017e: 26), well-identified priorities and already planned projects or activities would be supported to avoid an amplification of the economic crisis since public investments are normally cut down during a downturn. By assuring the continuance of investment projects, the Commission argues, permanent adverse effects on growth, employment and productivity could be prevented. Finally, private companies and households could overcome the crisis more rapidly and more robustly.

Rainy day fund

A third option suggested by the European Commission (2017e: 26) is a so-called rainy day fund which would be built-up gradually and could distribute its financial means to cushion a large shock. The disbursements from the fund would be limited strictly to its accumulated contributions. Consequently, in the event of a large shock its capacity might be too small. The Commission assumes that this problem could be solved if the fund would be equipped with the possibility to borrow[59].

5.1.3 Shifting sovereignty to European level: towards a fiscal union?

The two latter proposals need to be viewed in a broader context. When thinking of common budgets on euro area level that are possibly financed by national taxes and available for allocation to regions hit by asymmetric shocks, then the discussion is moving towards a fiscal union[60]. In fact, many observers demand further transfers of sovereignty from the national governments and parliaments to the European level as well as the introduction of a fiscal union, often associated with the creation of new institutions. Baldwin and Wyplosz (2015: 507), for instance, stress that the eurozone would need its own system of governance to improve its responsiveness to crises which currently would be too cumbersome. From their point of view, neither the Eurogroup nor the European Council was able to handle emergencies effectively and fastly enough. However, the propositions vary in both their understanding of the general approach and the concrete form. Some economists use equal terms, but a closer inspection reveals that they mean completely different things. In the following, the confusion will be disentangled.

A textbook example for this description is controversy over the establishment of a European Finance Minister. Schieritz (2017) points out that such a newly created position would be favored by many leading politicians[61], but that they would strongly disagree on the design. He explains that the German side would envision some kind of chief supervisor who could put a veto on new borrowing of a national finance minister, if he considers the additional debt excessive. This would be in line with the assumption that a major cause of the crisis was fiscal indiscipline and that proportionate public spending would at least lower the risk of another great crisis.

---

[59] Several proposals for common bond solutions will be discussed below.

[60] The scope of a fiscal union can be differently interpreted. For the purpose of this thesis, the definition of an IMF study (Allard et al. 2013: 6) on a potential fiscal union in the euro area will be adopted: a fiscal union, thereby, is considered "[...] *as a set of fiscal rules and arrangements, including possibly cross-country transfers, commonly agreed by euro area member states to deepen fiscal integration*".

[61] Schieritz names Emmanuel Macron, Angela Merkel and Wolfgang Schäuble.

The opposing side, however, is picturing a completely different institution. Bofinger (German Council for Economic Experts 2015: 40-42) proposes creating two new institutions: on the one side a Commissioner for Economic and Financial Affairs with the competence to initiate infringement actions at the European Court of Justice against eurozone countries that violate the rules; on the other side, a European Finance Minister being responsible for the economic and monetary policy in the EMU. The idea behind that is that an intergovernmental institution like the Economic and Financial Affairs Council (ECOFIN) cannot implement sanctions in a credible way. Bofinger assumes that a supranational institution equipped with the right to initiate procedures and to impose sanctions under the SGP, on the contrary, was able to bring together both joint liability and more effective sanctions. However, in his model the new institutions were not restricted to monitoring and vetoing the national finance ministers, but had fiscal stabilization functions at their disposal. He challenges the assumption that lower debt levels would enable the Euro states to make use of own, individual automatic stabilizers since this would disregard the fact that sufficient debt reduction would take decades in many countries. Furthermore, Bofinger criticizes that close cooperation of national fiscal policy was not adequately existent, therefore increasing the need for a common stabilizing function for the eurozone.

Enderlein and Haas (2015: 1) provide a more detailed concept of a European Finance Minister. According to their proposal, a European Finance Minister would safeguard the economic and financial interests of the Currency Union against the individual interests of the member states and had four main competences: (i) supervising the coordination of fiscal and economic policies; (ii) enforcing rules when they are violated; (iii) leading negotiations in crisis times; and (iv) contributing to buffering regional shocks. In order to fulfill his functions, he would be supplied with a European investment budget to counter-balance asymmetric shocks[62] and to reward structural reforms[63]. Moreover, he would preside the advanced ESM, called European Monetary Fund (EMF)[64].

---

[62] The authors (2015: 7-8) aim at avoiding that the government of a crisis-ridden state asks for more flexibility on the debt and deficit targets and intend that some of the additional expenditure should instead be absorbed by the European investment fund.

[63] Enderlein and Haas (2015: 8) advocate supporting early reform efforts through investments to mitigate negative effects on short-term GDP growth, thus making structural reforms more

In either way, creating the position of an Economic and/or Finance Minister of Europe would require changes to the current European Treaties since this institution would have the authority to influence public budgets (Baldwin, Wyplosz 2015: 507). Doubts can be raised whether a consensus is achievable that is likely to pass this high hurdle. Nonetheless, Allard et al. (2013: 17) formulate minimal elements for a fiscal union: in addition to a fiscal backstop for the Banking Union and some type of macroeconomic stabilizer (e.g. a rainy day fund or an EUBS), they deem joint borrowing and better oversight of fiscal policies[65] necessary to ensure stability in the euro area.

Gros and Mayer (2011: 1-4) also propose the introduction of a mechanism they call European Monetary Fund, but present a different idea than Enderlein and Haas. In order to create a support channel for member states in liquidity crises as well as to eliminate the diabolic loop, they recommend replacing the EFSF[66] with a European Monetary Fund which would contain two departments: The first would manage and finance adjustment programs and, if needed, facilitate orderly debt restructuring. The necessary funds would be backed by the member states. The second would react to liquidity gaps through intervention in the secondary market. It would be funded by own means and, if necessary, by ECB facilities. Hence, the EFSF (today it would be the ESM) would become a bank with access to re-financing by the ECB in case of emergency. Put differently, under this suggestion the ECB would become a LOLR. Gros and Mayer feel confident that their EMF would be an adequate liquidity backstop if a serious breakdown in confidence would occur. Even though they would prefer that the ECB had not to bailout this European rescue mechanism, they consider it the lesser of the two evils. Furthermore, they believe that their proposal would be conform to the European Treaties.

attractive. They state that the budget could be financed through a European tax or a reallocation of existing funds.

64 Both economists (2015: 8-10) identify several shortcomings of the current ESM and recommend to turn it into a European Monetary Fund with the ability to issue sovereign bonds. As already mentioned, common bond solutions will be examined below.

65 Allard et al. (2013: 17-19) inter alia propose letting the credibility of medium-term plans and any corrective measures of sovereigns evaluate by entrusting Fiscal Councils or other national independent agencies.

66 When Gros and Mayer presented their proposal, the EFSF was still in place and the ESM not existent.

De Grauwe (2015: 106-107) even goes as far as to claim that the Currency Union will not survive without a fiscal union. However, it is uncertain whether a majority can be found for such major integration steps anytime soon. De Grauwe identifies mutual distrust between the Euro states that would impede the necessary measures to build up a fiscal union, but there is more to bring forward. Fuest and Becker (2017: 214-217) acknowledge that a system of financial transfers could compensate for regional, asymmetric shocks, but believe that it would lead to permanent transfers from North to South[67]. Moreover, they urge that a compensation mechanism would set bad incentives: an EUBS, for instance, could entail postponements of unpopular labor market reforms. Another issue with respect to the feasibility of a fiscal transfer scheme such as a rainy day fund or an EUBS is the correct detection of the events triggering the scheme. Allard et al. (2013: 20) stress that there are technical methods to ascertain negative growth shocks, but indicate that they were not free of errors and complex to establish in real time, making it difficult to disentangle temporary from permanent shocks, and exogenous shocks from policy shocks. Moreover, they hint at the fact that any insurance mechanism entails the risk of "free-riding", which would be particularly true if the mechanism ends up delivering more permanent transfers than warranted: member states could be incentivized to build smaller fiscal buffers at the national level.

Beblavý et al. (2015: 14-15) admit that the risk of moral hazard is existent, but assume that either the introduction of a trigger, meaning the precise definition of an indicator and a threshold as trigger to determine when the transfers will be exercised, or a claw-back system could solve this problem. In the first mechanism permanent transfers could be avoided if the threshold was set high since then only severe recessions could trigger the EUBS. Secondly, Beblavý et al. recommend relating the indicator the rate of change of an indicator of economic activity and not on its absolute level. Thereby, they argue, all member states were likely to receive transfers at some point.

Gros and Mayer (2010) also note that the problem of moral hazard arises when mutualization of risks is established through any kind of mechanism or procedure. They concede that moral hazard cannot be abolished completely, but affirm that the design of their EMF version would limit it in two ways: on the one

---

[67] See part 2.1.1. with respect to transfers between member states.

hand, they stipulate that countries violating the Maastricht criteria had to contribute the main part. In their view, this could be achieved by setting the contribution rates as a combination of 1% annually of the amount of debt that exceeds the 60% debt-to-GDP ratio ceiling and 1% of the deficit that exceeds the limit of 3% of GDP[68]. The contributions, in turn, would be invested into sovereign bonds of fiscally strong eurozone member states. Euro countries with extraordinary strong public finances would not have to make payments, but would back the EMF and the high rate of their bonds in the EMF's portfolio. On the other hand, Gros and Mayer would link the disbursements from the fund to conditionality. They would allow any country to call on the funds of the EMF up to the amount it has contributed in the past (including interest), subject to the eurozone's approval of its fiscal adjustment program. If a country would need credit above this amount, any drawing on the guarantee of the EMF would be subject to a strict adjustment program supervised by both the European Commission and the eurozone.

Despite this argumentation, the GCEE (2015: 32-33) finds fault with a common fiscal policy at European level. Firstly, they highlight that the exact measuring of an asymmetric shock and the correct fiscal adjustment response is difficult. Production gaps, for instance, were hard to measure with sufficient precision. As a consequence, they see the danger of large redistribution effects in the shape of permanent unilateral transfers between member states. Secondly, fiscal transfers were not necessary since the adaptability to shocks could also be achieved through either capital and credit markets which calls for a further economic integration; or through own countercyclical fiscal policies what, however, requires reduction of debt levels to have leeway for fiscal measures. Feld and Osterloh (2013: 19) provide empirical evidence that the contribution of a fiscal capacity to absorb shocks in federations in which a fiscal union is implemented is relatively low. They claim that integrated capital markets better serve as an interregional risk sharing mechanism[69].

---

68 Both economists presume that the EMF would be able to borrow in the markets until its funds reach a certain amount. If it needs to do so, debt service would be financed with future contributions.

69 Feld and Osterloh (2013: 3) also note that the argumentation of supporters of a fiscal union is often closely linked to OCA theory. Remarkably, Robert Mundell, a founding father of the theory and an advocate of the Euro, postulates that it would not be recommendable to install

Apart from technical features and possible adverse effects, many economists doubt that a fiscal union is realizable at the moment. Having a centralized decision-making authority with fiscal competences would imply shifting national rights such as enforcing tax increases, spending cuts and structural reforms as well as influencing labor market and social policies to the European level. Feld et al. (2016: 4-5) think that a shift of sovereignty to this extent is not feasible due to the current cultural, political and economic differences. Allard et al. (2013: 21) agree on that and find that especially setting up some kind of euro area budget would require a far-reaching transfer of fiscal sovereignty which they consider unlikely to happen. Frankel (2015a: 436) states that more fiscal integration was inevitable in the crisis and was introduced via bond purchases by the ESM and the ECB. However, he believes that a full fiscal union was not enforceable in the short and medium term since Northern European voters were proven right with their fear that the introduction of the Euro would entail bailouts for Mediterranean countries.

Anxieties and resentments towards a fiscal union may be justified or not, but it cannot be denied that parliamentary control over budgetary matters is an essential element of democracies. Baldwin and Wyplosz (2015: 430-431) therefore emphasize that taking over control over the public budget of a country was a big step and that democratic legitimation of European institutions had to be given. It is on this point precisely that Fuest and Becker (2017: 142-143) believe that the necessary conditions are not fulfilled. In their opinion, a new central institution would lack legitimation which generally has to be gained by political (voters') support in a democracy. Hence, they are sure that a eurozone Finance Minister would soon be limited to symbolic functions as legislative competences would be treated with resistance. Baldwin and Wyplosz (2015: 431-432) add that finding and implementing a consensus on what is best for a country is very difficult which is why governments were reluctant to give away capacity for action in this respect.

a central European authority with the competence to largely intervene in the tax levels and spending of the member states (Welter 2013). From his point of view, the members of the Monetary Union had to find a formula to share, not shift sovereignty in exchange for transfers. According to him, a more sound solution would to focus on ensuring fiscal discipline of national states to avoid bailouts.

5.1.4 Enhanced macroeconomic coordination

The lack of macroeconomic supervision and coordination was tackled by implementing new and modifying existing regulations. These efforts, however, were not seen in an exclusively positive light (see section 4.1.). Nevertheless, Bourgeot (2013: 11-13) declares himself in favor of a further advancement of the macroeconomic coordination between European countries. In his view, such coordination was vital to the member states of a currency union. His analysis reveals that imbalances in the pre-crisis period could be traced back to inflation differences which he believes inter alia stemmed from considerably differing wage developments. He states that the German wage moderation was a key driving force and illustrates how differing wage setting can negatively influence the economic development of the whole Monetary Union. Hence, he concludes that it was of crucial importance to coordinate macroeconomic policies, especially with regard to wages. Thereby, not only the build-up of large imbalances could be prevented, but also the convergence process could be stimulated and competitiveness-enhancing measures could be supported.

In the Five Presidents' Report (Juncker et al. 2015: 8) Bourgeot's assumptions can be found again. Juncker et al. propose the introduction of independent competitiveness authorities being responsible for assessing whether wages are evolving in line with productivity and for comparing them with developments in other eurozone states and in the main comparable trading partners. They stress that these competitiveness entities would not aim at harmonizing practices and institutions in charge of wage formation across borders, but they would produce guidelines to be used by national actors during wage setting negotiations.

The GCEE (2015: 34-35), however, is of a different opinion: It disagrees with the claim that it would be realistic to assume that the wage negotiating parties would consider competitors in other member states. As a consequence, Euro states had to take care about their competitiveness themselves and implement the necessary reforms.

5.1.5 Dealing with the legacy debt problem I

The high debt-to-GDP ratios of several member states of the Currency Union form a major challenge themselves and additionally interfere with the reconstruction of the euro area. There are proposals how to deal with the legacy debt. Some of them imply more integration, some rather belong in the other category.

Corsetti (2015: 90) identifies three possibilities for countries to lower their debt in general[70]: (i) economic growth; (ii) increase of the trade surplus via (probably) economic and budget reforms; and (iii) restructuring of liabilities. Due to the extent of the legacy debt, he does not consider economic growth to be a realistic option. He states that both budget correction and debt reduction need two conditions: Some kind of backstop to public and/or private debt to prevent self-fulfilling speculative attacks on the one side, and institutions that set unambiguous and effective rules for handling solvency crises of both governments and private banks, in order to lower the costs and risks of contagion effect on the other side. For Corsetti (2015: 95-96) it is clear that the financial instability that grew in the eurozone after 2010 is mainly due to the lack of well-developed institutions on eurozone level that protect member states from self-fulfilling crises and correct the imbalances at the root of the instability. In his opinion, the main political hurdle to solve this problem was the widespread view that institutions and mechanisms that shield a member state from speculations would reduce the incentives to implement reforms and correct imbalances. He argues that this would be true for an insurance scheme which is likely to entail ex-post bailouts and transfers, but not for a pure backstop which would consist of a credible commitment to intervene in the event of a belief-driven speculative attack that threatens a country. He even claims that a backstop would increase incentives for reforms as the expected benefits from reforms in relation to their costs would be improved if a country was protected from arbitrary and destabilizing speculations.

A counterpoint could be that it may be difficult to distinguish between a fundamental and a belief-driven downturn. Moreover, Corsetti admits that it still was possible that private objectives of incumbent governments lead to false decisions. However, he is assured that well-developed eurozone institutions able to establish conditionality and strict rules that define what qualifies a nation for support, the backstop strategy could work. According to him, the ECB's OMT program addressed these requirements in many ways, but there was still

70 In other discussion papers, inflation is also listed as fourth option. As it already became evident, the inflation rates have changed in the eurozone. Riehle (2016: 253) criticizes that higher inflation fiscal stable member states combined with lower inflation in highly indebted Euro countries was equal to a transfer, with a bad outcome for savers and a good one for debtors. Corsetti (2015: 90), however, neglects that runaway inflation would solve the problem of excessive legacy debt.

institutional and policy uncertainty about banking union, fiscal rules, debt crisis governance and the general approach to consolidation. Another proposal was submitted by the GCEE and called European Redemption Pact (ERP). The GCEE (2012: 1-2) refers to the danger of a sudden loss in market confidence and therefore recommends securing the debt reduction initiated through the Fiscal Compact with further measures. In order to do so, the GCEE envisions a transfer of the share of the member states' debt above the 60% debt-to-GDP threshold into a European Redemption Fund (ERF). The liability for the ERF would be shared among the eurozone countries. In return, the participating member states had to dedicate themselves to payment obligations towards the ERF such that their transferred debt would be repaid within 20 to 25 years. Due to the joint guarantees private investors would have higher trust in the debt sustainability and refinancing costs for the respective states would decrease. This, in turn, would reduce primary balances and the debt ratios could be lowered more easily and safely. The participation of this ERP would be linked to strict conditionality, e.g. depositing collaterals. Moreover, the states had to commit to consolidation and structural reforms to ensure that debt does not exceed the 60% debt-to-GDP limit again. This means that debt brakes based on the German and Swiss models would be introduced in all member states. Countries going through an adjustment program should be able to join the ERP immediately, but the debt should only then be transferred if the adjustment program was successfully mastered.

In its Annual Report 2011/12 the GCEE (2011: 107-109) outlines that the legacy debt would not be transferred to the fund immediately, but within a roll-in phase of around five years. In this way, incentives for fiscal discipline would be created. Due to the crucial importance of compliance with the debt brake targets, they would be monitored by an independent European institution, for example by the European Court of Auditors. Violations of the national debt brake specifications would be sanctioned immediately with a penalty fee towards the ERF. Since the proposal is limited to eurozone states, the GCEE suggests using central bank seigniorage of the respective nation. In order to ensure the payments towards the Redemption Fund, participating countries had to commit themselves to establishing a markup on a national tax (e.g. added value tax) that would be used for repaying the fund. Moreover, it would be an option to write down in the national constitutions that payments towards the fund take precedence over domestic spending.

It should be highlighted that the proposal dates back to 2011/12. The introduction of debt brakes, for instance, became obsolete as they were implemented through the Fiscal Compact. Furthermore, the GCEE (2013: 147-148) itself states that the ERP was lapsed because of the OMT program of the ECB[71]. However, they believe that the ERP could still be an alternative, but not a complement to the OMT program. As the ERP has the same benefits as the OMT, but implies conditionality which is not the case for the ECB instrument, they do not expect the ERP to be established.

This position, however, is not shared by all members of the GCEE (2013: 149): Volker Wieland neglects the view that member states would not have an incentive for the ERP. By arguing that the OMT program will remain as permanent tool of monetary policy anyway[72], he concludes that exchanging OMT for ERP would be unreliable if initiated by the ECB. Nevertheless, the member states could still be interested in creating a redemption fund with joint liability.

Claessens et al. (2012) fault that it would be uncertain whether the countries will stick to the required fiscal discipline during this long period. If a member state would lack fiscal discipline or face an unanticipated increase in debt, the authors surmise that it had to cope with rising borrowing costs on the first 60% of the debt-to-GDP ratio. Thus, they question the practicability of the ERP. Brunnermeier et al. (2016: 1) add that the ERP would entail little degree of joint liability and also linked to strict conditionality, but that a union-wide safe asset would not be created under this concept.

5.1.6 Common bond solutions

It might be argued that any Eurobond solution is void due to the strong rejection in Germany and other countries[73]. In fact, other reform options seem more realizable in the current political and social environment. However, politics can

71 From the experts' point of view, the introduction of the ERP would have been better as the risks were lower relative to the OMT program. It would have been more explicit how public debt had to be decreased and which strict conditions had to be complied with. The GCEE criticizes that the ECB instead created a joint liability without linking it to a strict conditionality.

72 Even if OMT was terminated some day, Wieland believes that it could always be reactivated, if deemed necessary by the Governing Council of the ECB.

73 The German Chancellor Merkel, for example, stated in 2012 that Eurobonds would not be implemented as long as she lives (Watzlawek 2012).

change: The German opposition, for instance, is not as antipathetic to common bonds as the government (Schult 2017). Moreover, since his election, the new French President Macron generates new impetus in the debate on reforming the eurozone and also revitalizes the discussion on Eurobonds. He is likely to push forward his vision of a higher integration level for Europe and the chances are high that he is knocking on open doors. Eventually a new solution for the eurozone's architecture has to be found and in Germany the common sense that Macron should be supported is emerging[74] (Knauß 2017). So it does not seem absurd to consider that some sort of Eurobonds might be part of a future reform. Consequently, the current common bond proposals will be discussed[75].

Engler and Steffen (2014: 830) provide an overview over the debate and speak out in favor of objectifying the public discourse. In general, they think that common bonds would have three advantages: firstly, financial risks would reasonably be distributed. Secondly, through an improved and more robust integration of the capital markets financial stability would be enlarged. And thirdly, the international position of the Euro as reserve currency would be enhanced. Moreover, they indentify the need for a safe asset in the Monetary Union which would help balancing ex-ante and ex-post transfer payments. The latter point is an essential argument for supporters for common bond solutions: Brunnermeier et al. (2016: 1) believe that the diabolic loop problem could be solved with the creation of a safe asset since banks could store value in them and had not have to invest into risky sovereign bonds of their domestic government. Philippon and Hellwig (2011) also are assured that there is a huge demand for safe assets, especially in times of crisis. They trace this fact back to the BASEL III framework which imposed new liquidity ratios on banks which, in turn, bought government debt, irrespective of the sovereign's creditworthiness. If financial institutions could fulfill their liquidity requirements by purchasing a safe asset, they argue, the financial sector would be more stable. Bofinger (German Council of Economic Experts 2015: 40) agrees on that and stresses that the US, British or Japanese government bonds were viewed as 100% safe asset with respect to their

74 Analogous to Chancellor Merkel (see Part 1), Sigmar Gabriel, the German Foreign Minister, contended that "If Macron fails, we fail as well, and so does Europe" (Schult 2017).

75 It should be said in advance that the "classic version" of Eurobonds, meaning the mutualization of debt within the eurozone without any kind of conditionality or hedging, will not be considered.

nominal redemption amount. Thus, they would play a significant role for the stability of the respective financial system which in the euro area would be less robust to large-scale financial market shocks.

However, of course there are counter arguments: the main concern is moral hazard (Engler, Steffen 2014: 830-831). Sharing liability for jointly issued bonds may lead to excessive debt accumulation if the necessary incentives are not set[76]. Furthermore, Engler and Steffen urge that there were constitutional concerns as Eurobonds might require a fiscal union or even the creation of the Federal States of Europe. Another issue raised by the authors (2014: 834-835) is whether the status of common bonds should be senior or equal (pari-passu) to the national bonds.

The Blue Bond proposal

A highly regarded contribution to the Eurobond discussion is the so-called Blue Bond proposal which was submitted by Delpla and von Weizsäcker in 2010[77]. They (2010: 2) start from the trade-off arising out of the fact that, on the one side, low interest rates are desirable since they reduce the costs of government debt and thus lower the burdens for tax payers. On the other side, however, high interest rates are also desirable as early warning signal when a country is drifting away from a sustainable debt path. In their proposition, the two economists (2010: 2-4) attempt at achieving both: They suggest pooling the sovereign debt of all member states up to 60% of GDP in the form of a common European government bond with joint liability, which they name "Blue Bond". The debt which is exceeding the 60% would remain under national liability and be characterized by a subordinated status; Delpla and von Weizsäcker call this tranche "Red Bond". In the event of a partial default, the junior ('red') tranche would be hit first, while the blue tranche would only be affected when the whole amount of red debt was used already. As a consequence, the Blue Bonds would be less risky than the current sovereign bonds, while the red tranche would be more risky. By pooling and merging the blue tranches of all participating member

---

76 A system in which governments benefit from an easy access to cheap money, but simultaneously share the related risks meaning that possible costs will be distributed to all, is likely to tempt sovereigns to borrow in an exorbitant manner.

77 Since some years have passed since then, some of the framework conditions they demand may be partially existent already.

states, a government bond market similar in size, liquidity and quality to the US Treasury Bills market would be created. This would imply a significant liquidity gain that would further reduce the refinancing costs on the blue tranche. Contrarily, the liquidity of the red tranche would be significantly less than the liquidity of homogeneous status quo national bonds, what would further increase costs of borrowing on the red debt

Delpla and von Weizsäcker (2010: 4-5) outline several advantages of their common bond solution. They highlight that the main distinction between their proposal and other Eurobond ideas was the probable impact of the Red Bond on fiscal behavior. Fiscal discipline was likely to improve due to the increased cost of public-sector borrowing and would additionally reduce overall debt. Furthermore, the increased fiscal discipline would also lower the interest rates on the red tranche and, together with the liquidity effect on the blue tranche, it would ensure that the financing costs decrease on average relative to the current situation. Another benefit would be that the Euro could compete with the Dollar as a reserve currency since large public institutional investors, inter alia from Asia, greatly value liquidity and were likely to demand the Blue Bonds to a large extent. This again would probably lower the borrowing costs for eurozone member states[78]. In a later publication, both economists (2011: 1-4) point out that the Red Bonds should be widely kept out of the banking system in order to reduce systemic risk in the case of a sovereign bankruptcy. Thereby, the diabolic loop would be mitigated

In their papers (2010: 6-7), the institutional set-up is described as in the following: fiscal discipline would be strengthened through a differential allocation of blue bond borrowing quotas by member state. The higher the fiscal discipline in a country, the more blue bonds it would be allowed to issue with a maximum set at the 60% debt-to-GDP ratio threshold. If a country would lack sustainable fiscal policies, it would only allowed to borrow a lower proportion of GDP in blue bonds and may even be evicted from the mechanism.
Delpla and von Weizsäcker would create a so-called Independent Stability Council which would be responsible for distributing the blue bonds and which had to be convinced by the states with a weaker fiscal position to get access to the

[78] They (2011: 4) claim that in the US, the advantage from the large T-Bill market would amount to 0.8% of the nominal value per year and that in the eurozone the Blue Bond could yield an interest advantage of 0.3%.

mechanism and thus insurance in the form of joint liability by the most credible Euro states. The Independent Stability Council would propose an allocation which had to be approved by the national parliaments (Delpla, von Weizsäcker 2011: 2). If a country would neglect the allocation, it would not be able to issue blue bonds in the respective year, but neither be liable for the blue bonds of others. Hence, there would be a strong interest to keep fiscally stable economies inside the mechanism making the issuing of blue bonds beyond the 60% threshold highly unlikely. Nonetheless, through declining blue bond allocation it would be possible to remove member states that pursue an unsustainable fiscal strategy from the mechanism

Obviously, the Blue Bond proposal was developed thoroughly and addresses several of the discovered structural shortcomings of the Currency Union. However, some critical points can be found: Riehle (2016: 239-241) calculates that this mechanism would imply an interest rate disadvantage for Germany of 1.2% to 2.3% and thus a hidden transfer payment of €26 billion to €50 billion every year. With regard to this point, Delpla and von Weizsäcker (2011: 4) counter that this would only be correct if the whole eurozone debt would be pooled which is not the case for the Blue Bonds. Conversely, the interest rate for the blue tranche would be significantly lower since firstly, the Blue Bonds would only contain safe debt and secondly, would benefit from the liquidity gains.

Regardless of this dissent, Claessens et al. (2012) underline that sufficient demand for the red tranche would be essential, but uncertain. In their view, the value of Red Bonds would largely depend on the fiscal performance of the respective country and were subject to national fiscal shocks. A bond run in this tranche was possible and could then lead to similar conditions that protracted the current crisis.

Dübel (2011: 2) argues along a similar line. He puts focus on debt dynamics and claims that it would be possible or even typical that fiscally stable countries undergo a strong increase of debt above the 60% ceiling. He brings the cases of Ireland and Spain forward and states that these kinds of aggressive short-term government debt dynamics were not exceptional cases, but would occur regularly and were highly probable to end in default. In a crisis, sovereign debt levels would rapidly amount into the red tranche which is why it could be questioned whether static GDP limits for public debt should be used as predictor for sovereign financial stability. Dübel believes that Euro states would seek more rapidly for help from the ESM, which would be an issuer of Blue Bonds and thus would be able to pass on most of its interest rate advantages. In the end, he thinks that financial markets would anticipate the ineffectiveness of Red Bonds during a crisis and would consider both Red and Blue Bonds to be fully backed by the ESM. This, however, would result in the vanishing of market discipline.

Partial insurance system

Consequently, Dübel (2011: 3) provides an alternative proposal. Instead of the Blue Bond model, he favors a partial insurance system covering both principal and interest by the ESM. The form of partial insurance he envisions would equip the protected bond with a passive senior-junior structure that would be activated if the bond insurance is called. In this case, the principal and interest of the junior bond would not be protected by the ESM. The trigger date would be when the borrower applies to the ESM to act as LOLR. Moreover, the non-maturing bonds would be split into a tradable junior bond and a senior bond to be serviced by the ESM as planned. The tradable junior bond would enable a better management of the balance sheet risks of investors and could be sold to investors interested in speculative assets. Junior bonds could be restructured (e.g. with payouts linked to growth) or defaulted under the fiscal adjustment program to be set between the ESM and the affected country. The governments that participate in the ESM scheme would receive comprehensive control rights in return for their partial sovereign bond guarantee. Different insurance premiums to fund the mechanism should be determined by using fiscal policy criteria.

Dübel (2011: 4) identifies the fact that investors would still be provided with explicit crisis risk protection, but the negative effects from having a static debt-to-GDP threshold would be abolished as main advantage of his proposal. He assumes that marginal cost of funds would be reduced significantly, especially during crisis. Furthermore, he states that the value of debt would be different from the Blue Bond proposal[79]. As a result, incentives for fiscal discipline would also be created for the range below 60%, which is not the case for Blue Bonds. Increasing

[79] Dübel explains that, under the Blue Bond proposal, the value of debt would always equal the par value of debt below the 60% threshold, meaning that no sovereign risk premium is charged. As soon as the debt level exceeds the 60% ceiling, implying that additional debt is based on individual liability, the additional market value of the additional debt would be significantly below its nominal value. The marginal bond interest rates would surge and accelerate the financial distress. This would be very different with the partial insurance mechanism: capital markets would always price in risk, that is, also at low debt levels (under 60%), causing that the value of debt would always be under its par value.

debt would also lead to higher risk premiums since markets would charge a higher interest rate for the rise in probability of the bonds being split. However, this increase in marginal bond prices would be considerably lower relative to the increase between Blue and Red Bonds, thus leaving leeway for debt reducing measures. The probability of initiating the ESM proceedings in times of crisis (debt-to-GDP above 60%) will thus be far smaller.

In concrete terms, Dübel (2011: 6) suggests setting the ratio of the junior part between 40-60%. When the mechanism was triggered, the junior bond would become subordinated to both the senior bond it was split from and all subsequently issued bonds. Together with the affected government, the ESM had the power to change the conditions of maturity, amortization and interest rate to support the fiscal adjustment program of the borrower. The senior bond tranche would be amortized by the ESM under its normal conditions without further conditionality what only would lead to public discussions and thus political risk. In this way, a floor under investors' losses was created and a crucial capacity of investors' liquidity needs was safeguarded. Dübel emphasizes that this would be of major importance to avoid bottomless senior bond prices and illiquid markets and hence instability in the bond market as a whole. Investors could sell the junior bond or keep it to its restructured maturity. Consequently, he expects sufficient demand for such securities. In his concluding remarks (2011: 7-9), he highlights that it would be crucial not to split junior and senior debt at the beginning since this would diminish risk monitoring incentives of senior bond-holders. Moreover, the ECB as well as the ESM would require a larger scope for purchases. Finally, he claims that, additionally to the insurance premiums and guarantees given, further automatic capitalization mechanisms such as ring-fencing of EU-wide VAT revenue might be necessary.

Mayer (2013: 140-141) reviews this proposal and arrives at the conclusion that Dübel's partial insurance mechanism would not lead to false incentives for borrowers as it would be the case with a joint liability for debt. He assumes that there would be more certainty about the remaining value of the claims towards sovereigns in case of insolvency, as investors could more easily determine their expected maximum losses (the non-insured part of debt times the insolvency probability). As a consequence, spreads would again reflect the solvencies of the member states and could make evaluations easier. For both creditors and borrowers costs would emerge, but only to a limited extent. Hence, the breakdown of financial system could be prevented.

European Monetary Fund with the ability to borrow in the markets

In section 5.1.3. the proposals of Gros and Mayer as well as Enderlein and Haas were presented. Both teams of authors suggest creating a European Monetary Fund, although they differ in the modeling. Besides the name of their idea, they have another parallel line, namely that the EMF should be able to borrow in the markets. While Gros and Mayer do not submit further specifications, Enderlein and Haas (2105: 9-10) elaborate the mechanism. Under their proposition, the EMF would issue sovereign bonds up to a limited level of e.g. 10% of GDP which would be guaranteed by the euro area countries. The interest rate would be equal for all. Thereby, a liquid and safe financial asset would be created that Enderlein and Haas deem qualified to also mitigate the diabolic loop. In their view, another advantage would be that in normal times, the remaining debt would be issued on national level, hence spreads would remain. When refinancing costs would increase enormously (due to economic crisis or changes in market sentiments) in a member state, it would be allowed to issue additional bonds through the EMF, subject to a pre-determined gradual transfer of sovereignty. The guiding principle would be that more financing implies more external control. Furthermore, the two economists would install a possibility to react to non-compliance with the obligations by stopping the issuance of debt through the EMF of the respective member state. As a result, restructuring of its national debt was likely to be needed which is why Enderlein and Haas recommend the introduction of an insolvency mechanism[80].

Eurobills

Quite a similar approach is presented by Philippon and Hellwig (2011) who propose the creation of what they call "Eurobills". Under their suggestion, a European debt agency named Debt Management Office (DMO) would be created and issue short-term common debt with maturity of less than a year (the Eurobills). The eurozone member states would not issue individual short-term bonds, only sovereign bonds with a maturity of two years or more. Each quarter, the DMO would issue an amount of Eurobills covering the needs of the eurozone

80 Establishing an insolvency mechanism is widely discussed among economists and politicians. However, as an insolvency scheme would imply more individual responsibility and maybe even less integration to some extent, the debate on this issue will be examined in section 5.2.1.

countries. The level of outstanding Eurobills was limited to 10% of GDP at any point in time[81]. For this amount, however, joint and several liability would be granted by the participating countries. If the Eurobills do not face enough demand, the ECB would step in and retain the unbid amount. The member states then had to repurchase the amount within one quarter. If a member state would not be able to meet its obligations, the other countries had to help out. In order to get access to the Eurobills mechanism the member states had to fulfill criteria of economic governance and budgetary discipline.

Philippon and Hellwig describe the rationale behind their proposition as follows: The objective was to prevent self-fulfilling liquidity runs and the negative feedback between government and banking crises, while simultaneously keeping the risk of moral hazard minimal. Eurobills would neither render improved governance and fiscal discipline dispensable nor increase the overall amount of short-term debt, but would only replace existing short-term bonds. By giving up the right to issue short-term bonds on their own, countries would make Eurobills effectively senior to all other liabilities that the member states issue. Eurobills would increase financial stability and thereby reduce costs of long-term borrowing. Both credible seniority and strict limitation of the issuance amount should convince strong countries to accept the joint and several liability. Due to the joint liability, the authors are convinced that Eurobills would be as safe as the short-term bonds of the most liable borrower and even more liquid. They expect that, in times of crisis, Eurobills would protect member states with fundamentally sustainable fiscal policies from contagion.

With regard to moral hazard problems, they stress that it was crucial to ensure that Eurobills are senior to other debts. In this respect, shortening the maturity of the contracts would help as this implies that Eurobills had to be rolled over at least once a year, which gives more negotiation power to the agency responsible for fiscal surveillance. Finally, they consider the simple and transparent structure of Eurobills as advantage since it would thereby be easier to estimate the costs of implicit guarantees. This was particularly true in comparison with proposals based on tranching and more complex financial structures.

81 Philippon and Hellwig refer to the USA as role model, where short-term US T-Bills represent about 10% of GDP.

The latter issue meets with great approval by Claessens et al. (2012) who believe that the short maturity has the potential advantage of enforcing continuous discipline. Moreover, they believe that Eurobills could be compliant with the European Treaties. In general, they consider a gradual development from Eurobills to Blue Bonds as realistic. Brunnermeier et al. (2016), however, criticize that Eurobills imply a joint issuance of short-maturity bills of up to the amount of 10% of a nation's GDP.

Synthetic Eurobonds

Contrarily, in the proposal of Beck et al. (2011) joint liability is not embedded. The authors start from the diabolic loop problem and submit a solution they call "synthetic Eurobonds". Analogously to the Eurobills model, Beck et al. envision the introduction of a new centralized institution: A European debt mutual fund would purchase a mixture of the debts of the Euro states according to pre-determined proportions (e.g. GDP). The fund would issue tradable securities, the so-called synthetic Eurobonds, of which the payoffs would stem from the payoffs of the sovereign bonds held in the fund's portfolio[82]. The major advantage would be that synthetic Eurobonds would not imply joint guarantees or bailouts among member states. Synthetic Eurobonds would not be entirely risk-free, but due to the diversification drastic reductions in payments would be unlikely. If Greece, for instance, would default on its debt, Beck et al. calculate that the pay-off of the synthetic Eurobonds would be affected, but only up to the extent of the Greek share in the fund's portfolio (2%, if GDP was used).

A key factor would be the ECB's acceptance of the synthetic Eurobonds as collateral in their open-market and repo operations while simultaneously refusing to accept bonds from fiscally weak member states. In this way, the ECB would stop being exposed to sovereign default risk and the rich countries would also benefit as they would not have to guarantee sovereign debt of other member states in order to save the banking system.

Engler and Steffen (2014: 831-832) explain that synthetic Eurobonds do not encompass joint liability, but rather aim at securitizing existing sovereign debt in order to create a safe financial product. Hence, unlike other common bond

82 Beck et al. define the pay-off of the synthetic Eurobonds as the sum of the interest rate payments of the sovereign bonds held by the fund.

solutions, synthetic Eurobonds would not have the primary objective to finance public budgets or to safeguard crisis-stricken countries from speculative attacks. Instead, the main target was to mitigate the interconnectedness of banks and states such that prospects of default do not lead to a vast decrease of the market value of the affected sovereign debt, subsequently threatening the solvency of some banks. Brunnermeier et al. (2016: 1) criticize that the synthetic Eurobonds model would not include tranching which they consider crucial for the degree of safety of the bonds.

European Safe Bonds

Brunnermeier et al. (2012: 3-4) prefer a solution they call European Safe Bonds[83] (ESBies) which would be create and issued by a European Debt Agency (EDA) in compliance to the existing European Treaties. On the one hand, the economists aim at solving the diabolic loop by implementing a safe asset. On the other hand, they have the target of preventing that capital flows from the center to the periphery in normal times when investors look for higher yields, and from the periphery to the core countries in crisis times, when investors seek for safe havens[84]. They argue that flight-to-safety capital flows would not be characterized by cross-border movements anymore, if ESBies were introduced.

The structure and use of ESBies would be designed such that the EDA was in charge of purchasing national sovereign bonds according to fixed proportions that reflect the relative size of the different member states (Brunnermeier et al. 2012: 4-6). It would be prohibited to modify the proportions as reaction to a crisis. The EDA would hold the government bonds as assets in its balance sheet and use them as collateral to back the issuance of two securities that divide the debt in a senior and a junior tranche[85]. The ESBies would include the senior claim to the

---

[83] Bauer et al. (2011) present a similar proposal which they call structured Eurobonds. Their idea is equal to ESBies except for two aspects: firstly, they include more than two tranches; secondly they envision a trust fund which would be equipped by common financial means. Hence, it would imply partial liability which is not the case for ESBies.

[84] Brunnermeier et al. are bothered about large capital account imbalances in the eurozone and possible disruptions in asset markets which may be generated by these movements. Moreover, they elucidate that capital flowing from unsecure countries to fiscally stable member states deteriorates the situation in the capital loosing countries.

[85] The tranching is considered to be a key aspect for the safety of ESBies which is why the researchers believe that ESBies should be preferred to synthetic Eurobonds (see above). In another publication, Brunnermeier et al. (2016) illustrate with numerical simulations that the safety of ESBies is enhanced when tranching and pooling interact.

payments from the bonds held in the EDA's portfolio. Up to a certain limit, this tranche would not be affected by a default of sovereign debt. This limit would be expanded by collecting initial capital from the member states that would be used as additional guarantee. In this manner, a very safe asset would be created[86]. The second securities, called European Junior Bonds (EJBies), would contain the junior claim to the payments from the eurozone member bonds. Losses had to be borne by the investors; neither ESBies holders nor other member states had to bail out the defaulting state. In the junior tranche ESBies had a risky counterpart what could yield that capital flows from EJBies to ESBies and not across borders in a crisis[87].

Brunnermeier et al. link the success of the ESBies to two regulatory modifications. First of all, the ECB had to grant strict preferential treatment to ESBies by accepting them as the primary form of collateral in repo and discounting operations. As a consequence, the ECB would only indirectly hold sovereign bonds as assets and also only the safest part of these government bonds. Secondly, in terms of banking regulation, the ESBies had to be given a zero risk weight, which should not automatically be the case for other government bonds. As a result, risks of sovereign bonds were reflected correctly.

The authors (2012: 11-12) are convinced that, given that the regulations are implemented, ESBies were safe for three reasons: firstly, pooling of sovereign bonds would reduce the risk of default since it was improbable that all governments get insolvent at the same point of time. Secondly, in combination with tranching, meaning that there is a senior tranche of the portfolio that grants the right to be paid off first, pooling was even more effective and would make ESBies significantly safer than German bonds. Finally, additional guarantee in form of a fund that is financed upfront and used to absorb losses in case that the default exceeds the size of the junior tranche would make the ESBies even safer. Eventually, banks could invest into ESBies and thereby diversify more easily, resulting in less dependency on their nation's public finances. As a result, not only the adverse flight-to-safety capital movements, the dysfunction of the no-bail-out clause and the absence of a safe asset, but also the diabolic loop were tackled. In a

---

86 The economists emphasize that ESBies would not imply joint and several liability.

87 Brunnermeier et al. (2012: 20) regard this as decisive advantage over the Blue Bond proposal.

later contribution, Brunnermeier et al. (2016: 6-7) point up some additional aspects: for instance, they state that the tranching point at which the junior part is subordinated to the senior part could be set at 30%. Then, the junior tranche would represent 30% and the senior tranche 70% of the underlying nominal value and were fully collateralized by the sovereign bond portfolio. Ultimately, they feel assured that there would be sufficient demand for the junior bonds due to their embedded leverage and expected loss rate which would be similar to the today's bonds of fiscally weak eurozone states.

Claessens et al. (2012) find many advantages of the ESBies concept. They appreciate that ESBies would not require a fiscal union and that the proposal does not deal with new issuance of sovereign bonds, but implies repackaging of existing bonds traded on the secondary market. Consequently, no sovereign guarantee was needed. Moreover, they consider it realistic that ESBies would decrease the probability of multiple equilibria and instability. Engler and Steffen (2014: 836-837) add that the creation of a central safe haven by issuing common bonds would bring about the crucial advantage that average and marginal interest rates on public debt could be differentiated more easily. The average interest rates would be lower by virtue of safe-haven-benefits and the liquidity premium, while the marginal interest rates would reflect national circumstances and thus differ from each other. Thus, they conclude that if the pricing of national bonds was not biased by other influences, strong incentives to improve the quality of national economic policies and not to disregard long-term sustainability were set.

However, Claessens et al. (2012) also remark that the ability to attract buyers for the EJBies was essential for the success of the model. This point is shared by the GCEE (2016: 273-274) which raises doubts about whether there will be adequate demand for EJBies in crisis periods and if the issuance of ESBies would then be possible. The experts acknowledge that the argument that flight capital would not move cross-border was reliable and praise that the implementation of ESBies would mean creating a safe asset while simultaneously maintaining market discipline and without introducing a joint and several liability for risks. However, they urge that it could not be excluded that the ECB would find itself forced to purchase EJBies due to insufficient demand. Therefore, fully restoring market discipline would be unlikely. They arrive at the conclusion that through securitization risk could not be reduced but only redistributed, requiring the continuation of the consolidation process.

5.2 Proposals including more individual responsibility and/or less integration in the eurozone

In section 5.1. it was illustrated in detail that there are many ideas and also concrete models how to reform the euro area's architecture such that the design flaws are offset and the Currency Union becomes robust to future (asymmetric) shocks in whatsoever form. However, it also became evident that these proposals are not only opposed due to specific, technical features, but that some observers hold a fundamentally different opinion.

In general, this opposing side considers fiscal discipline of the member states as key aspect for the stability in the Monetary Union and doubts that fiscal moral hazard can be eliminated through a strengthening of the rules. Advocates of this view point to the fact that clear rules and transparent sanctions have been available ever since, but were repeatedly violated. Hence, they ask why this should be different in the future. Most of them believe that it is wrong on the one side and impracticable on the other to shift more competences to already existing or newly created institutions, in particular when it comes to the usage of public funds and the power to influence taxes. As explained in section 5.1.3., having control over a national public budget is seen as one of the most precious assets of a democracy and therefore requires democratic legitimation. Consequently, concerns are raised whether European institutions should be equipped with responsibilities in this area and moreover, if national populations would accept this kind of supranational interventions in times of crisis. Put differently, developing the eurozone into a fiscal union is rejected by this side. At least it is believed that a far-reaching fiscal union is not realizable in the current political and social environment.

Additionally, some economists are obviously convinced that the economic roles in the Currency Union are clearly defined for the time being. Therefore, they assume that introducing cross-border stabilizers on European level would certainly end up in one-way permanent transfers from the fiscally strong to the weak member states. Furthermore, such mechanisms would lower the pressure on governments to implement necessary structural reforms and thereby reinforce that giving and receiving positions were carved in stone.

Another issue mentioned is that self-commitments of national governments made on European level would often lack credibility. Fuest and Becker (2017: 135-136) find that politicians would frequently disassociate themselves from tediously elaborated agreements of various EU and Eurogroup summits when returning to their home country and facing national actors such as voters, the press or opposition parties. Being liable to their voters would complicate representing unpopular eurozone-level decisions in their state which resulted in a recurring non-compliance of these resolutions. Consequently, Fuest and Becker identify an inability of the euro area to determine credibly and long-lasting unpopular political measures.

So what the supporters of the just outlined beliefs demand is that liability and control must not diverge in order to ensure that fiscal moral hazard behavior affects not the collective, but solely the performer of profligate spending or excessive risk taking. According to their argumentation, if national governments could and maybe should not be curtailed in their decision-making power, reforms should arrange that governments were exclusively accountable for their actions and could not rely on others to bear their costs. Basically, this was equal to revitalizing the no-bail-out clause which indeed is called for by many economists.

5.2.1 Insolvency mechanism

A concrete measure for the reunification of liability and control is the implementation of a eurozone-wide insolvency procedure implying that losses from a sovereign default had not to be borne by the other member states, but by its creditors only. As indicated before, some of the economists that favor more integration in the euro area propose connecting their solutions to an insolvency scheme. This applies to Enderlein and Haas (2015: 9-10) who reserve reactions to non-compliance with the obligations of their EMF model which they consider likely to necessitate a restructuring of sovereign debt. For this case, they recommend establishing an insolvency mechanism such that restructuring of debt would not be equal to exiting the euro area. Gros and Mayer (2011: 3) not only call for an EMF as well (even if differently designed; see above), but would also implement an insolvency statute to enable an orderly debt restructuring. Same holds true for Engler and Steffen (2014: 830) who support the realization of a common bond solution, but state that disciplinary market effects were necessary to prevent excessive debt levels. Hence, they link the success of any Eurobond type to the parallel introduction of an insolvency procedure.

Among German economists, the integration of an insolvency mechanism has much appeal as well: Riehle (2016: 222-223) highlights that it would be common that states fail and get bankrupt, thus a having instruments to orderly deal with this were requisite and could lower effects on third-party states as well as prevent a delayed filing of insolvency. Interestingly, also Jens Weidmann shares this view and calls for some kind of insolvency scheme (Zydra 2016). For Sinn (2017), it is a matter of course that investors who purchase sovereign bonds should not be able to rely on taxpayers of other states to help out if a crisis occurs. He even adds that if such an insolvency mechanism had been in place, the capital markets had purchased less sovereign bonds and the inflationary bubbles that caused low competitiveness levels would not have emerged in the first decade of the Monetary Union

Fuest and Becker (2017: 157) believe that a realignment of the debt control was inevitable. Instead of issuing new provisions for the borrowers, they think that it would be more expedient to focus on the creditors who would still lend money to highly indebted states and seemed to still be relying on an implicit bail-out promise in the Monetary Union. They expect that by means of new regulations for sovereign bankruptcy, these disruptions could be eliminated. This assumption meets with the GCEE's (2015: 29-30) approval: the experts deem appropriate to contemplate the ESM by an insolvency mechanism implying that sovereign debt had to be restructured before access to ESM funds was granted. In their opinion, an insolvency mechanism for governments would both help with burden sharing and crisis prevention. Furthermore, fiscal discipline would be enhanced since investors would be incited to carefully assess a nation's default risks and to translate them into risk premiums. However, an insolvency code including a bail-in rule could set incentives for governments to borrow even more, which is why it was to be flanked by a macroeconomic adjustment program that corrects these negative incentives. Ideally, an insolvency framework should determine binding rules and establish criteria that initiate insolvency proceedings quasi-automatically. The automatic character of the insolvency mechanism would avoid political negotiations and decrease uncertainty such that market participants can adjust their expectations accordingly. The equal treatment of all creditors had to be ensured such that there is neither a "rush to the exit" nor a holdout problem. The automatism should be according to a debt-to-GDP threshold[88].

[88] In its Annual Report of 2013, the GCEE (2013: 161-162) outlines a framework with three relevant ranges for the case of a liquidity crisis in a member state: if the debt-to-GDP ratio was below 60%, the respective government should get rapid access to ESM means. If the ratio was between 60% and 90%, access would only be granted subject to conditionality.

However, the GCEE admits that introducing an insolvency procedure oriented at a certain debt-to-GDP threshold (e.g. 90%) was difficult. It refers to the high public debt levels in the eurozone and deduces that the mere announcement could cause serious disruptions on the capital markets. On the other side, the economists intimate that postponing the implementation of an insolvency mechanism would make it difficult to avoid the involvement of taxpayers in a next financial crisis. Thus, it would be preferable to decide on insolvency proceedings now and to gradually implement them in order to not cause turmoil on capital markets. In the event of a debt crisis and the suspension of a nation's capital market access, the ESM was in charge of conducting a debt sustainability analysis to determine whether a return to a sustainable debt level could be achieved through financial assistance (including conditionality) or only via debt restructuring (e.g. through extension of existing bonds or a complete debt restructuring).

As already indicated, however, it seems difficult to implement an insolvency scheme without taking major risks. Fuest and Becker (2017: 157) concede that a way must be found such that the consequences of insolvency were manageable. The rising refinancing costs would be problematic for many member states, but also for banks which would have to adjust the value of their stock of sovereign bonds. The GCEE (2013: 162) urges that creating insolvency proceedings could be followed by withdrawal of funds by creditors of fiscally weak member states which would deteriorate the strained economic situation.

Its member, Peter Bofinger, once again delivers a dissenting view on the subject. He (German Council for Economic Experts 2015: 40) believes that if an insolvency mechanism was introduced even minor shocks could trigger an unstoppable bond run as investors had to assume that public debt would always be restructured as soon as a member state was exposed to pressure on the capital markets. Moreover, the mechanism would take away the option to make use of high government deficits to mitigate a severe recession which would be crucial when it comes to a crisis, as the example of the 2009/10 response to the economic downturn showed when an anti-cyclical fiscal policy was used to prevent a repeat of the Great Recession. Hence, he concludes that an insolvency framework would

---

Finally, if the debt level was above 90%, the respective country would only get funds from the ESM if its debt was restructured with a bail-in of private investors and also if it agreed on a macroeconomic adjustment program.

weaken the stability of the eurozone by increasing the risk of default of the member states' sovereign bonds. A fiscal union, by contrast, would be the right step to be taken.

5.2.2 Exit option

Integrating an insolvency mechanism into the Currency Union's architecture would definitely shift more responsibility to the individual governments and thereby impose more pressure as well as restore the no-bail-out clause. An even more drastic proposal is the idea to create a regulation that allows for an exit from the euro area. The discussion arose during the crisis, especially when the Greek government repeatedly refused to implement stipulated reforms. In 2015, Wolfgang Schäuble brought a temporary exit option up for discussion when the negotiations with Greece were deadlocked (Eddy 2015). So far, there is no legal fundament that sets rules for leaving the Currency Union (see section 2.2.4.2.), but there are calls for changing the Treaties accordingly. One rationale behind this request is that there is no toolset for handling a stubborn member state that constantly steps out of the line and rejects carrying out necessary political and economic actions. The case of Greece is considered a prime example in this respect: when the new left-wing government was elected, it annulled the agreements between its predecessor and the other Euro states and demonstrated an obstructive mentality (Bernau 2015).

Sinn (2014: 21-22) argues that the disruptions stemming from the eurozone's design flaws can only be remedied with permanent transfers between the member states or exits[89]. In his view, permanent transfers could not be the solution since they would not lead to more competitiveness, but to the Dutch Disease, contagion effects upon states that strive for the same treatment and fixation of the wrong price vectors. The only option to restore competitiveness without riots and conflicts was to exit from the Currency Union and to afterwards devaluate the new currency. Sinn finds empirical evidence showing that countries that do so improve significantly within one or two years. No member state should

[89] It should be mentioned that a possible exit of a member state would require clarification with regard to its claims or liabilities within the TARGET2 system. In a letter to two members of the European Parliament, Mario Draghi announced that *"If a country were to leave the Eurosystem, its national central bank's claims on or liabilities to the ECB would need to be settled in full"* (Draghi 2017: 2). In any case, the TARGET2 balances would become a bargaining chip in possible withdrawal negotiations.

be forced to exit the eurozone, but staying in the Monetary Union while taking for granted that the other countries will permanently finance the deficits was neither acceptable.

The former President of the Ifo Institute for Economic Research (2014: 23-24) envisions a set-up in which a member state deciding to leave the euro area would be supported by the other Euro countries to achieve an orderly process. Social burdens resulting from the recapitalization of banks would be lowered by using debt-equity swaps. Basic services and energy provision would be supported with common funds to compensate for the expected increase in import prices. In any case, there would be a return option for the exiting country which would remove the stigma of a permanent separation. The European Exchange Rate Mechanism II (ERM II) could be used for re-entering the Monetary Union. Since the pure announcement of exiting from the Euro would cause turmoil and contagion, the new currency had to be prepared in secret and implemented over a weekend when the banks are closed. All deposits and all contracts between domestic partners denominated in Euros such as labor contracts, rental contracts or pensions would be converted immediately into the new currency while keeping the numerical values. The new currency would rapidly face devaluation pressure, but once it was regaining stability, the country could join the ERM II. The re-entry should be subject to an agreed reform agenda.

If an exit plan was leaked, Sinn expects bank runs to occur and demands that they should then be stopped with capital controls. Furthermore, he admits that the conversion was hard to realize, but proposes allowing the Euro as a parallel currency in the exiting country. In this way, transaction could still be made in Euros, but would immediately be converted. As a consequence, there would be no point in hoarding Euros or capital flights.

Sinn (2014: 25-26) identifies the fact that the foreign debt of the existing country would still be denominated in Euros as a major problem. However, he states that, with respect to foreign debt, there was no difference between an internal depreciation through wage and price cuts and an external depreciation after implementing a new currency. Depreciation, however, was the only possibility to develop a structural current account surplus even though this comes along with an initial rise in the debt ratio, independently of whether internal or external depreciation is chosen. Furthermore, he counters the argument that the exiting country would face inflation of an extent which would eliminate the positive effects from depreciation by explaining that inflation would only occur if the depreciation went too far such that prices were below their equilibrium levels.

The GCEE (2015: 32) is also in favor of introducing an exit option in the euro area. One reason, among others, for the lack of an exit procedure was that a country leaving the eurozone could cause speculation about the remaining member states. However, the experts also point to the Greek crisis and emphasize that it would be indispensable that the Euro states cooperate under the terms of an adjustment program. Otherwise, the Monetary Union's fundament could be undermined to an extent threatening the Euro's existence. Hence, an exit from the eurozone had to be possible as ultima ratio, although in an orderly way and accompanied with economic support to avoid a humanitarian catastrophe. Feld et al. (2017: 5-6) add that this would prevent hesitations and the need for the ECB to jump in, thereby loosening its independency.

Fuest and Becker (2017: 225) demand a demystification of the Euro which, in their view, should not be seen as a major step of European integration and be separated from the question of war and peace. They seek for a paradigm shift: as there were different ideas of how to manage a currency it should be possible to voluntarily resign from the Euro without having an anti-European stigma afterwards.

Having an exit option is not part of the current political discussion. One reason is that the consequences of a country leaving the Monetary Union are uncertain. In 2015, Barry Eichengreen stated that a Greek breakaway would be a catalyzer akin to the bankruptcy of Lehman Brothers in the World Financial Crisis (Robb 2015). Among politicians it was feared that if one country would leave the eurozone, speculative attacks against others would emerge and bring the whole euro area to the brink of the abyss (Herwartz 2015). The Economist (2014) elucidates that the decision-makers of the euro area around Angela Merkel thought about introducing an exit option, but always arrived at the conclusion that it would be more expensive than keeping the Monetary Union together. Most probably, the strongest argument was and is that the European leaders consider the Euro as described by Fuest and Becker, namely as major step of European integration, which is why no country should be thrown out.

5.2.3 Accountability Bonds

Many criticism and opposition was raised towards common bond solutions. Fuest and Heinemann (2015) challenge the view that debt mutualization should be the answer to the specific insolvency risk. They acknowledge that individual states were protected from belief-driven speculative attacks of market investors by the ECB's OMT program, but stress that the price was huge: The interest rates for highly indebted member states had decreased to a level that did not reflect the fundamentals of these countries. The interest rate reduction had been a welcome relief for many member states, but this step had rewarded excessive debt accumulation and penalized countries that had made efforts to improve their economic performance and to have sustainable public debt levels. The authors urge that the nearly complete interest rate convergence was similar to pre-crisis situation when the disappearance of spreads had contributed significantly to the developments leading to the crisis. As a result, necessary reforms were postponed and the eurozone would face the peril of repeating the same mistake.

According to Fuest and Heinemann, the implementation of so-called Accountability Bonds could be an appropriate alternative: Governments that would not comply with the debt and deficit rules had to issue parts of their debt as Accountability Bonds. If a country would trigger the ESM program or exceed a determined debt limit (e.g. 120% debt-to-GDP), these bonds would default. Temporary exceptions could be made for member states that currently have a high debt level. The two economists assume and approve that the capital markets would start assessing countries based on their financial and economic decision-making. This mechanism would complement the reformed SGP by introducing automatic, market-based sanctions if the debt rules were violated. In order to maintain or, respectively, restore the ECB's independency, it would not be allowed to purchase them. Finally, Fuest and Heinemann disclose that they are convinced that debt mutualization should neither be existent for the first 60% of debt, which is why they prefer their solution to the Blue Bond proposal.

Together with Johannes Becker, Fuest (2017: 157-158) further elaborates his suggestion. They present the Accountability Bond solution as alternative to an insolvency mechanism which they approve, but simultaneously view critical with regard to its feasibility (see section 5.2.1.). Their Accountability Bonds would comprise a clause that determines that these bonds lose their value (partially or completely), e.g. if the ESM program was requested. Thereby, the normal roll-over of debt would not be affected. An irregular budgetary deficit in economic normal times, contrarily, could only be financed with these subordinated bonds that would be expensive for the states as investors would charge high risk premiums. A prerequisite would be that the banking regulation would set a severe limit for the Accountability Bonds hold by banks. In the event of a crisis, an exception would apply: new borrowing could then be made with primary bonds what would have the effect of a macroeconomic stabilizer.

In concrete terms, Becker and Fuest envision that the European Banking Authority (EBA) and the ESM would collect statistics about sovereign bonds that were issued above the deficit limit, define them as subordinated and treat them accordingly in the event of a rescue program. There would not be any political committee involved in order to abolish the self-commitment problem. Consequently, the risk would be with the creditors, not with the other member states. This would raise the interest rates for capital above the debt limit and hence set incentives not to do so.

Ettel et al. (2017) identify approval for the proposal, but indicate that it would be crucial under which national law the Accountability Bonds would be issued. It would be essential to ensure that the conditions for the Accountability Bonds could not be altered by decree.

5.2.4 Dealing with the legacy debt problem II

In section 5.1.5. it became clear that the high debt levels in the eurozone are a great problem which is difficult to handle. So far, the approach has been to impose austerity stipulations on the overindebted member states in the hope that trade surpluses would emerge and the countries would grow out of their debts. This strategy already follows the principle of more individual responsibility. Proposals how to accelerate the process tend to deviate from the latter and rather imply sharing costs. Fuest and Becker (2017: 199-209) review several options and find that the plan to make no new deficits, but create economic growth and use surpluses for debt reduction would take too long. However, they do not discover an optimal alternative solution. Sinn (2014: 9) favors a European debt conference to negotiate an appropriate mixture of debt relief, privatization and wealth levies in order to reduce the debt of crisis-ridden states. He believes that additional hard budget constraints would exacerbate the crises in the GIPSIC countries. Finally, he (2014: 18) arrives at the conclusion that there should be an honest debt restructuring implying debt relief and an economic strategy with more private saving as well as investment and less consumption. Put differently, even Sinn doubts that the legacy debt problem can be solved without sharing costs among the member states. This would not necessarily have to be categorized as an increase in integration, but could even less be equated with more individual responsibility.

6 Assessment

How can the euro area crisis be solved in the long run? This is certainly one of the most pressing questions in Europe, but finding an answer is difficult and complex. Nonetheless, today is the best time to think about major reforms for the eurozone. As pointed out before, the discussion was stimulated by the election of Emmanuel Macron who pushes forward the debate on long-term solutions for the Monetary Union. Moreover, due to rising anti-European parties such as the Front National in France, a consensus is emerging in Germany that the French President has to be supported in order to prevent his failure which could possibly be followed by coming into power of the radical Front National. Additionally, 2017 is also an election year in Germany which implies that the probability of unpopular, substantial changes is increasing once the poll is done. Hence, it is no surprise that the French and German Finance Ministers initiated a German-French working group with the assignment to develop proposals in this subject area (Bundesministerium der Finanzen 2017b).

It became obvious that the discussion can be divided into two main camps which disagree on the underlying causes of the crisis and therefore draw different conclusions with respect to the previous countermeasures and the further steps to be taken. Those who believe that the member states' dependency on irrationally behaving capital markets is the essential factor argue in support of more integration and inter-eurozone compensation mechanisms. Contrarily, the opposing side is convinced that macroeconomic fundamentals are the key aspect both in the pre-crisis period and today. Hence, they suggest finding ways to ensure that governments again become liable for their actions implying that incentives for fiscal discipline were set and protection against profligate behavior was established.

Both sides present strong arguments for their points of view. It cannot be denied that some member states borrowed excessively without taking their deteriorating competitiveness into account and thereby brought themselves into a vulnerable and weak position. Fiscal discipline does play an important role which is why it is reasonable to think about reforms that set stronger incentives for moderate public spending. Having a closer look at the debt-to-GDP ratios of the Euro countries before the crisis, however, reveals that fiscal discipline is only one part of the story and that it is possible that thrifty sovereigns also may be pushed into liquidity crises and rapidly surging debt levels. Belief driven, self-fulfilling vicious circles can happen to any country, in particular when it faces adverse consequences from past economic decisions. It cannot be excluded that Germany or France are the next states discovering that there has been a real estate bubble evolving and thus face an asymmetric shock that provokes distrust of investors.

This argumentation inevitably leads to the finding the modification of the Monetary Union's architecture should contain solutions of both categories. In fact, the opposing sides could come to an accommodation by mutually accepting proposals: Advocates of the creation of a safe asset, for instance, could assert their idea by approving an insolvency mechanism. A reform package including a selection of measures that stem from both camps is not only most expedient, but also most probable.

Such a basket of measures should fulfill the following requirements: first and foremost, a solution for the legacy debt problem must be found. There is a consensus among the economists that especially Greece is not likely to grow out of its debts. However, the high debt levels hamper both recovery and structural reforms on European level and therefore must be approached. Secondly, as just described, fiscal discipline is of great relevance for the prevention and handling of crises, but needs to be flanked by a mechanism that protects the member states from speculative attacks which are very dangerous due to specific insolvency risk. The ESM seems to be insufficient, both in terms of capacity and alignment, which is why further steps need to be taken. Thirdly, if possible, the ECB should be discharged from purchasing sovereign bonds. Announcing the OMT program significantly helped stabilizing the euro area, but the concerns with respect to its independency are valid. The fourth requirement is that, in any case, solutions must not lead to permanent transfers within the eurozone. One consequence, among others, is that mutualization of debt with joint and several liability should, if at all, be introduced to a very limited extent. Fifthly, it is assumed that countries cannot be forced to implement necessary but painful reforms – at least not without political damage[90]. The crisis has shown that some member states, despite being net borrower and unable to repay, were in a rather strong negotiating position since it was clear that the European decision-makers were unwilling to let a member state fall[91]. This should be changed. However, it is

90 By referring to the case of Greece where the Troika was widely perceived as intruder, this viewpoint is backed with strong arguments.

91 The absence of a formal way to kick a member state out of the Monetary Union may have contributed.

unlikely that increasingly strict rules and harsh sanctions will do the job since the enforcement remains weak. Moreover, even if a consensus was found today that existing or newly created eurozone-level institutions should be equipped with far-reaching control and intervention rights, the future practicability was still uncertain. Political conditions and social moods can swiftly change as the recent examples of the USA or Turkey, but also Hungary and Poland demonstrate. Who knows how to handle a eurozone member that suddenly refuses to implement specifications made by the collective? The ball should not be in the corner of the other member states which had to solve a problem that cannot be tackled in a satisfactory way. Thus, if a country was continuously unwilling to meet its obligations or too indebted, it should be possible to let it default on its debt without having major impacts on the rest of the euro area[92]. Sixth and finally, the diabolic loop must be eliminated.

The analysis and the requirements should be translated into a solution that provides those member states with a strong safety net which commit themselves to fiscal discipline as well as compliance to the rules and credibly promise to support the Currency Union. On the other side, it should be ensured that countries that stray from the common path are liable for their own actions and cannot hold the other nations hostage. This, however, is easier said than done. Arranging a combination of feasible and effective measures which can be implemented without leading to a significant surge in costs for all or some or single member states without entailing undesirable economic developments in the eurozone is not realistic.

Corsetti et al. (2016) propose a three-part model which can be seen as attempt to find a workable combination package. The first pillar would be a sovereign debt restructuring regime in which insolvency would be defined through a debt sustainability analysis and which would abolish leeway for discretion to delay restructuring. The creation of a safe asset such as ESBies would be the second pillar. Thereby, the diabolic loop problem was tackled. Finally, a stability fund would be introduced that would purchase the debt exceeding 90% of debt-to-GDP

---

92 Another underlying assumption that underlines this point is that national politicians primarily represent national interests and that their main objective is to be reelected. Hence, especially in election years they are likely to postpone unpopular reforms. While many decisions on European level are medium-term oriented, national politicians rather focus on the short run.

of each member state. In order to finance these purchases, the stability fund would issue debt collateralized by capitalized future fiscal payments of the participating member states which would also give a guarantee to the stability fund. To ensure the credibility of this commitment, revenues generated at eurozone level, seigniorage for instance, or additional wealth or VAT taxes would be used. The ECB would provide liquidity if necessary.

Naturally, the success of a proposal like this one would be uncertain, but it would comprehensively deal with the remaining problems and comprise inputs from both camps. The general structure is well selected and should be used as point of orientation. Instead of introducing a stability fund, the ERP suggested by the GCEE or even a debt haircut could be chosen. In return, an insolvency scheme[93] should be brought into being to achieve that capital markets would better price in risks and thereby impose more pressure on the governments to spend their public budgets carefully. Moreover, it could more easily be dealt with constantly recalcitrant member states. Integrating an exit option as alternative or as complement had several advantages, but is far from being realistic. The demanded demystification of the Euro is not going to happen and therefore the possibility of a partial breakaway from the Currency Union will not be realized. There are definitely valid reasons why it is not smart to closely link means of payments with the future of a continent. It was shown more than once that economic laws cannot be levered out by political will. Ignoring economic principles then leads to huge costs that, in turn, may have negative feedback effects on politics. However, separating the Euro from politics is not realistic as the intension of creating the Euro was primarily political and not economic. Moreover, it can be mentioned that the European Union was already founded as European Coal and Steel Community, hence using an economic unification as political adhesion to pacify and to promote the continent lies in the roots of Europe. There is little evidence that this is going to change, so it should be concentrated on increasing individual responsibility by an insolvency mechanism and not by an exit procedure.

The third component would be the creation of a safe asset. Part 5 illustrated that there are many proposals how to design such a security, but they all have critical points. The rationale behind the Blue Bond model is well-founded, but the doubts

---

93 According to the framework outlined by the GCEE (see section 5.2.1.).

concerning its practical implementation are justified. Dübel's alternative, the partial insurance, solves some of the disruptions, but it is uncertain whether shifting far-reaching control rights to others in the event of a crisis can be carried out without causing resentments and political conflicts. So generally, it seems more reasonable and also more universally acceptable to focus on a common bond solution that does not imply joint and several liability. Starting with a concept such as ESBies, structured or synthetic Eurobonds would mean lower risk and could still be extended. Through the introduction of a safe asset, liquidity shortages were less probable and the diabolic loop could be mitigated. Additionally, the ECB could probably refrain from purchasing sovereign bonds since a safe asset had sufficient demand also in crisis periods. Nevertheless, additional measures should be taken into consideration: the adverse interconnection between sovereigns and their domestic banks should be resolved by new banking regulations forcing banks to pursue a better diversification. The risk of liquidity crises degenerating into solvency crises stemming from the specific insolvency risk could further be reduced by augmenting the ESM. In general, more attention should be given to the idea of establishing pre-crisis funds that can be used when a crisis occurs (see section 5.1.2.3.). Implement a hybrid solution such as the EMF proposed by Gros and Mayer is also conceivable. It is true that it is difficult to accurately distinguish liquidity and insolvency conditions, to exactly measure an asymmetric shock and to determine the correct fiscal adjustment response. Hence, the GCEE is right in making aware of the resulting danger of permanent unilateral transfers. Further research is required in this area, but the basic approach of collecting funds in good times to build up a buffer for economic downturns should be both familiar[94] and taken into consideration. Thereby, not only means were available on European level which would ensure that every member state would have at least some capacity for automatic stabilizers, but the euro area community also had also a bargaining chip at its disposal when negotiating with reluctant governments. Possible costs for the collective arising from selfish behavior of an individual member could partially be paid by these funds.

A mechanism like this should be given preference over a concept that implies a major shift of sovereignty to the European level. As already explained, a transfer

94 See Keynesianism.

of far-reaching competences is probably not capable of winning a majority and even if it was, it would still be uncertain whether control and intervention rights would be effective. However, since it is of crucial importance that supervision is fully operative when sharing risks and potential costs, it should be desisted from propositions as the EUBS.

Finally, the excessive imbalance and competitiveness differences need to be tackled. To some extent, it needs to be accepted that the European Union and the euro area consist of heterogeneous countries that differ in their economic potential. The remaining deficits gradually have to be reduced. Progress in this respect is visible. The criticism being made of the German export surplus is vigorously countered by several German economists[95] and there are plenty of indications that they have sound reasons to find fault with the MIP's characteristics. Basically, macroeconomic coordination between sovereign states is complicated and the prospects of success are limited. However, having increased transparency and attempting to carry out arrangements and coordination to the greatest possible extent is advisable and can at least lead to earlier warnings than it was the case before the current euro area crisis evolved. Hence, the European Semester should be refined, but continued.

The convergence of competitiveness is being approached by several initiatives on European and international level[96]. In principle, it is gratifying to have an enhanced awareness of the potential consequences of massively diverging member states and to counteract such developments on a supranational level. However, the competitiveness of an economy and its robustness to shocks overwhelmingly remains a national responsibility. It is mainly up to national politicians to provide the necessary conditions for their domestic economies to develop in a prospering way.

In summary, a package of reforms leading to more integration in some areas, but simultaneously shifting more responsibility to individual governments would be the best solution to remedy the design flaws of the Euro's architecture and to base

95 See for example: Fuest and Becker (2017: 99-107), GCEE (2014: 218-221 and 2015: 34).

96 In this context, the Euro Plus Pact should be mentioned. Moreover, the European Commission (2017b: 10-11) addresses this issue in its current reflection paper and suggests further steps to diminish the competitiveness differences. Sigmar Gabriel suggest the creation of a German-French investment fund to foster the financing of infrastructural projects, R&D and other areas (Müller et al. 2017: 18).

the Monetary Union on a stabilized fundament. Strong mutual support should be hedged with escape options if the debt level of a country becomes too high or a government continuously refuses to stick to the agreed rules and conventions.

7 Conclusion

The European Union is going through an eventful and turbulent time. It is enormously challenged by, among others, drastically changing conditions in terms of foreign policy and the refugee crisis. Another urgent task is to agree on reforms that eliminate the construction faults in the architecture of its common currency. Major efforts were necessary to prevent the break-up of the euro area during the crisis that was triggered by the Great Recession of 2007. Until today, the adverse effects of the mistakes that were made before and after the introduction of the Euro are still perceptible and require extensive countermeasures. However, it is clear that the current set of measures is not sufficient to change the deficient status quo and to push the eurozone on a sustainable, long-term oriented path. Despite this knowledge and a wide range of proposals, there is no consensus on how to reform the Currency Union. Hence, this thesis aimed at disentangling the confusing discussion and at answering the question "how can the euro area crisis be solved in the long run?".

For this purpose, it was started with detecting the origins of the crisis. In order to get a broader understanding of the mechanics of monetary unions, the OCA theory was presented. It establishes criteria that should be fulfilled by all countries before founding a currency union. Obviously, the member states did not meet the requirements which was known and influenced the structuring of the Euro. By means of the convergence criteria, the SGP and the no-bail-out clause the founding fathers attempted to compensate the shortcomings. However, it became evident that they failed and that the member states significantly diverged in their economic performances and built-up large imbalances in the first years after Euro was launched.

The underlying causes for this development as well as for the escalation of the situation after the World Financial Crisis hit the eurozone are controversially discussed. One side emphasizes the lack of fiscal discipline that had brought the crisis-stricken states into their weak position. The other side focuses on the so-called specific insolvency risk which would leave the euro area countries at the capital markets' mercy, independently of their macroeconomic fundamentals. Both sides demonstrate valid arguments and there is strong evidence that both viewpoints are necessary to correctly describe the characteristics of the Monetary Union. In any case, the crisis management was complicated by the absence of a rescue architecture, the diabolic loop which resulted from inadequate banking supervision and political conflicts of interests which altogether contributed to the escalation of the slump.

In a second step, it was examined which countermeasures were taken to regain control and to remove the construction errors. Thereby, three main areas were determined: macroeconomic measures, monetary policies and the creation of the Banking Union. Based on this overview, controversial points were reflected and it was assessed to which extent the rescue efforts have solved the identified key problems. It was explained that in particular the ESM as liquidity provider and the unconventional monetary policy measures of the ECB were viewed critically and even led to legal proceedings. Nevertheless, it was concluded that the application of these measures was inevitable to react to the deteriorating situation even though the raised concerns were sound, especially in the context of the ECB's independency. In an interim conclusion, the open issues that still need to be remedied were analyzed, inter alia including the danger of belief driven speculative attacks, the unsolved diabolic loop and the lack of credible incentives for fiscal discipline.

Afterwards, selected proposals that deal with these unresolved problems and their related criticism were summarized. Accordingly to the examination of the roots of the crisis, the propositions were divided into two categories. On the one hand, the suggestions implying more economic integration were grouped together. In this camp, mostly supporters of the opinion that the specific insolvency risk was the predominant factor which should be taken into account when reforming the euro area could be found. On the other hand, the proposals aiming at less integration or at least imposing more responsibility on individual governments were listed. Here, the prevailing assumption was that fiscal discipline would be the key factor to stabilize the Currency Union. Therefore, ways had to be detected how to ensure that the member states spend their financial means carefully and, if they do not, how to manage that the costs are not loaded onto the others.

The presented ideas for further integration steps encompassed reforms like a Europe-wide deposit insurance scheme to complement the Banking Union and macroeconomic stabilizers such as a European unemployment benefit mechanism. Together with others, the latter concept was put into a broader context, namely the formation of a fiscal union which is envisioned by many economists and politicians. However, misgivings about implementing a system in which the member states shift national competences to the eurozone or European level to jointly decide on public spending were highlighted. Other suggestions in this category cover macroeconomic coordination between the Euro countries, the legacy debt treatment which is indispensable due to current high debt-to-GDP ratios and the options to introduce a common bond solution. It was stressed that the Eurobond debate is not void because, among other things, it was revitalized in the course of the election of the new French President Emmanuel Macron. Objectifying the discussion is desirable since common bonds could entail great benefits, but analyzing the most popular models such as the Blue Bond proposal or European Safe Bonds evinced that all of them imply risks.

Thereafter, the side questioning that more integration should be introduced and instead calls for abolishing the divergence of liability and control was reviewed. It became clear that advocates of this request doubt that stricter fiscal rules and sanctions are sufficient to achieve a paradigm shift in a sense that excessive borrowing on the expense of others can be excluded in the future. Moreover, they believe that a major transfer of competences to the European level is neither realizable nor preferable. Naturally, also minor modifications of treaties or small regulations can contribute to making governments more liable for their actions. Nonetheless, there are two far-reaching propositions how to credibly reach this target: introducing an insolvency mechanism and/or an option for exiting the euro area. Both ideas are criticized, but integrating an insolvency scheme into the Euro's architecture is also induced by economists who are in favor of advancing economic integration in the Monetary Union.

Finally, it was outlined how a comprehensive answer to this thesis' question could look like. In the end the eurozone should be reformed by drawing on advices from both factions. However, neither major transfers of sovereignty nor implementing an exit option seem feasible. It is more recommendable to agree on a reform package that is oriented towards the three-part solution of Corsetti et al. (2016). Combining a measure that tackles the legacy debt with an insolvency mechanism and the creation of a safe asset would yield that governments face more pressure to prevent excessive borrowing, but may resort to a safety net that prevents the escalation of a liquidity crisis.

Further research is required in many fields since all proposals imply risks and potential adverse effects which should be ruled out to the highest possible extent. Regardless of technical features, it should be highlighted that the feasibility of all solutions largely depends on what the European people are willing to accept. In this respect, more empirical evidence should be gained as well.

Bibliography

Acharya, Viral (2012): Banking union in Europe and other reforms, http://voxeu.org/article/banking-union-europe-and-other-reforms, (24.05.2017).

Afxentiou, Panos C. (2000): Convergence, the Maastricht Criteria, and Their Benefits, in: The Brown Journal of World Affairs, 7 (1), p. 245-254.

Albertazzi, Ugo / Ropele, Tiziano / Sene, Gabriele / Signoretti, Federico M. (2012): The impact of the sovereign debt crisis on the activity of Italian banks, in: Bank of Italy Occasional Paper, 133, Rome: Bank of Italy.

Allard, Céline / Brooks, Petya K. / Bluedorn, John C. / Bornhorst, Fabian / Christopherson, Katharine / Ohnsorge, Franziska / Poghosyan, Tigran (2013): Toward a Fiscal Union for the Euro Area, https://www.imf.org/external/pubs/ft/sdn/2013/sdn1309.pdf, (10.06.2017).

Baldwin, Richard / Beck, Thorsten / Bénassy-Quéré, Agnès / Blanchard, Olivier / Corsetti, Giancarlo, de Grauwe, Paul / den Haan, Wouter / Giavazzi, Francesco / Gros, Daniel / Kalemli-Ozcan, Sebnem / Micossi, Stefano / Papaioannou, Elias / Pesenti, Paolo / Pissarides, Christopher / Tabellini, Guido, Weder di Mauro, Beatrice (2015): Rebooting the Eurozone: Step I – agreeing a crisis narrative, London: CEPR Press.

Baldwin, Richard E. / Wyplosz, Charles (2015): The Economics of European Integration, 5th ed., London: McGraw-Hill Education.

Barroso, José M. D. (2011): Speech by President Barroso: "A Europe for all weathers", http://europa.eu/rapid/press-release_SPEECH-11-838_en.htm (18.05.2017).

Bauer, Christian / Herz, Bernhard / Hild, Alexandra (2011): Structured Eurobonds, Trier: Research Papers in Economics.

BBC (2015): Irish banking crisis inquiry: Ireland was 'pushed' into bailout, http://www.bbc.com/news/world-europe-33185690, (08.06.2017).

Beblavý, Miroslav / Marconi, Gabriele / Maselli, Ilaria (2015): A European Unemployment Benefit Scheme. The rationale and the challenges ahead, Luxembourg: Publications Office of the European Union.

Beck, Thorsten / Wagner, Wolf / Uhlig, Harald (2011): Insulating the financial sector from the European debt crisis: Eurobonds without public guarantees, http://voxeu.org/article/eurobonds-without-public-guarantees-insulating-financial-sector-european-debt-crisis, (14.06.2017).

Bénassy-Quéré, Agnès (2012): The case for a synthetic Eurobond, http://www.eurointelligence.com/news-details/article/the-case-for-a-synthetic-eurobond.html?cHash=b158e8e07e4ce8ce7fcd8ad88e18e28f, (14.06.2017).

Bernau, Patrick (2015): Griechenland kippt Euro-Einigung, http://www.faz.net/aktuell/wirtschaft/eurokrise/griechenland/griechenland-kippt-euro-einigung-beim-finanzminister-treffen-13423598.html, (16.06.2017).

Bild (2010): Ihr griecht nix von uns!, http://www.bild.de/politik/wirtschaft/keine-hilfe-fuer-griechen-11706824.bild.html, (23.05.2017).

Blanchard, Olivier / Giavazzi, Francesco (2002): Current Account Deficits in the Euro Area: The End of the Feldstein-Horioka Puzzle?, in Brookings Papers on Economic Activity, 2, p. 147-186.

Bongardt, Annette / Torres, Francisco (2017): EMU as a Sustainable Currency Area, in: Nazaré, Costa C. / Gonçalves, José R. / Cunha Rodrigues, Nuno (Eds.): The Euro and the Crisis. Perspectives for the Eurozone as a Monetary and Budgetary Union, Cham: Springer International Publishing.

Bourgeot, Rémi (2013): Labour Costs and Crisis Management in the Euro Zone: A Reinterpretation of Divergences in Competitiveness, Paris: Foundation Robert Schumann.

Bundesministerium der Finanzen (2014): Fragen und Antworten zum Stabilitäts- und Wachstumspakt, http://www.bundesfinanzministerium.de/Content/DE/FAQ/2011-08-16-stabilitaets-und-wachstumspakt-faq.html (29.05.2017).

Bundesministerium der Finanzen (2017a): Europäische Finanzhilfen im Überblick, https://www.bundesfinanzministerium.de/Content/DE/Standardartikel/Themen/Europa/Stabilisierung_des_Euro/europaeische-finanzhilfen-im-ueberblick-pdf.pdf?__blob=publicationFile&v=14, (25.05.2017).

Bundesministerium der Finanzen (2017b): Gemeinsame Presseerklärung von Wolfgang Schäuble und Bruno Le Maire, http://www.bundesfinanzministerium.de/Content/DE/Pressemitteilungen/Finanzpolitik/2017/05/2017-05-22-PM15.html?pk_campaign=Newsletter-05.2017&pk_kwd=22.05.2017_Gemeinsame+Presseerkl%C3%A4rung, (17.06.2017).

Bundesverfassungsgericht (2014): Urteil des Zweiten Senats vom 18. März 2014, - 2 BvR 1390/12 - Rn. (1-245), http://www.bverfg.de/e/rs20140318_2bvr139012.html, (01.06.2017).

Bundesverfassungsgericht (2016): Leitsätze zum Urteil des Zweiten Senats vom 21. Juni 2016, 2 BvR 2728/13, 2 BvR 2729/13, 2 BvR 2730/13, 2 BvR 2731/13, 2 BvE 13/13, https://www.bundesverfassungsgericht.de/SharedDocs/Downloads/DE/2016/06/rs20160621_2bvr272813.pdf;jsessionid=17456EA908BFF5DCFCA95CD0168C2731.1_cid361?__blob=publicationFile&v=5, (04.06.2017).

Broz, Tanja (2005): The Theory of Optimum Currency Areas: A Literature Review, in: Economic Trends and Economic Policy, 104 / 2005, p. 53-78.

Brunnermeier, Markus K. / Garicano, Luis / Lane, Philip R. / Pagano, Marco / Reis, Ricardo / Santos, Tano / Thesmar, David / Van Nieuwerburgh, Stijn / Vayanos, Dimitri (2012): European Safe Bonds (ESBies), https://personal.lse.ac.uk/vayanos/Euronomics/ESBies.pdf, (24.05.2017).

Brunnermeier, Markus K. / Langfield, Sam / Pagano, Marco / Reis, Ricardo / Van Nieuwerburgh, Stijn / Vayanos, Dimitri (2016): ESBies: Safety in the tranches, https://www.esrb.europa.eu/pub/pdf/wp/esrbwp21.en.pdf, (13.06.2017).

Cœuré, Benoît (2013): Outright Monetary Transactions, one year on, https://www.ecb.europa.eu/press/key/date/2013/html/sp130902.en.html, (30.05.2017).

Corden, Warner M. (1972): Monetary Integration, Essays in International Finance, Princeton: Princeton University Press.

Corsetti, Giancarlo (2015): Roots of the Eurozone crisis: Incomplete development and imperfect credibility of institutions, in: Baldwin, Richard E. / Giavazzi, Francesco (Eds.): The Eurozone Crisis: A Consensus View of the Causes and a Few Possible Remedies, London: Centre for Economic Policy Research.

Corsetti, Giancarlo / Feld, Lars / Koijen, Ralph / Reichlin, Lucrezia / Reis, Ricardo / Rey, Hélène / Weder di Mauro, Beatrice / Giugliano, Ferdinando (2016): Reinforcing the Eurozone and Protecting an Open Society, http://www.lucreziareichlin.eu/Content/_Documents/Reinforcing%20the%20Eurozone%20-%20MEZ%202%20-%20April%202016.pdf, (24.05.2017).

Council of the European Union (2005): Presidency Conclusions, Brussels: European Council.

Council of the European Union (2017): Single Resolution Mechanism, http://www.consilium.europa.eu/en/policies/banking-union/single-resolution-mechanism/, (31.05.2017).

De Grauwe, Paul (2015): Design failures of the Eurozone, in: Baldwin, Giavazzi (Eds.): The Eurozone Crisis. A Consensus View of the Causes and a Few Possible Solutions, London: CEPR Presse, p. 99-108.

Deutsche Bundesbank (2015): Geld und Geldpolitik, Frankfurt: Bundesbank.

Deutsche Bundesbank (2017): TARGET2-Saldo, https://www.bundesbank.de/Redaktion/DE/Standardartikel/Aufgaben/Unbarer_Zahlungsverkehr/target2_saldo.html, (19.06.2017).

Deutscher Bundestag (2010): Scheitert der Euro, dann scheitert Europa, https://www.bundestag.de/dokumente/textarchiv/2010/29826227_kw20_de_stabilisierungsmechanismus/201760.

Dombret, Andreas (2017): Die Niedrigzinspolitik der EZB – Fluch oder Segen für Wirtschaft, Verbraucher und Banken?, https://www.bundesbank.de/Redaktion/DE/Reden/2017/2017_02_01_dombret.html#doc390972bodyText6, (04.06.2017).

Draghi, Mario (2017): Letter to Mr Marco Valli and Mr Marco Zanni, https://www.ecb.europa.eu/pub/pdf/other/170120letter_valli_zanni_1.en.pdf?be6aea5c0aa3596d1d08149b510ea707, (19.06.2017).

Eddy, Melissa (2015): Germany's Tone Grows Sharper in Greek Debt Crisis, https://www.nytimes.com/2015/07/17/world/europe/eurozone-greece-debt-germany.html?_r=0, (16.06.2017).

Eichengreen, Barry (1990): One money for Europe? Lessons from the US currency union, in: Economic Policy, 5 (10), p. 117-187.

Engler, Philipp / Steffen, Christoph (2014): Sichere Anleihen für die Währungsunion: Stärkung des Bailout-Verbots durch ein stabileres Finanzsystem, in: DIW Wochenbericht, 36, 827-837.

Ettel, Anja / Tauber, Andra / Zschäpitz, Holger (2017): Top-Ökonom schlägt Sünden-Bonds für Europa vor, https://www.welt.de/finanzen/article162087078/Top-Oekonom-schlaegt-Suenden-Bonds-fuer-Europa-vor.html, (16.06.2017).

European Banking Authority (2017): The Single Rulebook, http://www.eba.europa.eu/regulation-and-policy/single-rulebook, (31.05.2017).

European Central Bank (2010): Monthly Bulletin. June 2010, https://www.ecb.europa.eu/pub/pdf/mobu/mb201006en.pdf, (30.05.2017).

European Central Bank (2012a): Monthly Bulletin. March 2012, https://www.ecb.europa.eu/pub/pdf/mobu/mb201203en.pdf, (29.05.2012).

European Central Bank (2012b): Verbatim of the remarks made by Mario Draghi. Speech by Mario Draghi, President of the European Central Bank at the Global Investment Conference in London
26 July 2012,
https://www.ecb.europa.eu/press/key/date/2012/html/sp120726.en.html, (30.05.2017).

European Central Bank (2012c): Technical features of Outright Monetary Transactions, https://www.ecb.europa.eu/press/pr/date/2012/html/pr120906_1.en.html, (30.05.2012).

European Central Bank (2015): Annual Report 2014, Frankfurt: European Central Bank.

European Central Bank (2016): What are minimum reserve requirements?, https://www.ecb.europa.eu/explainers/tell-me/html/minimum_reserve_req.en.html, (30.05.2017).

European Central Bank (2017a): More details on the Eurosystem's corporate sector purchase programme (CSPP) – Questions & answers, https://www.ecb.europa.eu/mopo/implement/omt/html/cspp-qa.en.html, (30.05.2017).

European Central Bank (2017b): Annual Report 2016, Frankfurt: European Central Bank.

European Central Bank (2017c): Asset purchase programmes, https://www.ecb.europa.eu/mopo/implement/omt/html/index.en.html, (30.05.2017).

European Commission (2015a): The Euro Plus Pact. How Integration into the EU Framework can Give New Momentum for Structural Reforms in the Euro Area, https://ec.europa.eu/epsc/sites/epsc/files/strategic_note_issue_3.pdf, (29.05.2017).

European Commission (2015b): Proposal for a REGULATION OF THE EUROPEAN PARLIAMENT AND OF THE COUNCIL amending Regulation (EU) 806/2014 in order to establish a European Deposit Insurance Scheme, http://eur-lex.europa.eu/legal-content/EN/TXT/PDF/?uri=CELEX:52015PC0586&from=EN, (31.05.2017).

European Commission (2015c): Updated version of first memo published on 15/04/2014 - Banking Union: restoring financial stability in the Eurozone, http://europa.eu/rapid/press-release_MEMO-15-6164_en.htm?locale=en, (31.05.2017).

European Commission (2016a): Making it happen: the European Semester, http://ec.europa.eu/europe2020/making-it-happen/index_en.htm, (25.05.2017).

European Commission (2016b): Stability and Growth Pact: fiscal proposals for Spain and Portugal, Brussels: European Commission.

European Commission (2016c): Quarterly Report on the Euro Area, 15 (3), Luxembourg: Publications Office of the European Union.

European Commission (2017a): Europe 2020 strategy, https://ec.europa.eu/info/strategy/european-semester/framework/europe-2020-strategy_en, (25.05.2017).

European Commission (2017b): The EU's economic governance explained. An explanation of the EU's economic governance, https://ec.europa.eu/info/sites/info/files/eu-economic-governance-explained.pdf, (29.05.2017).

European Commission (2017c): Single supervisory mechanism, https://ec.europa.eu/info/business-economy-euro/banking-and-finance/banking-union/single-supervisory-mechanism_en, (31.05.2017).

European Commission (2017d): Excessive imbalance procedure, https://ec.europa.eu/info/business-economy-euro/economic-and-fiscal-policy-coordination/eu-economic-governance-monitoring-prevention-correction/macroeconomic-imbalance-procedure/excessive-imbalance-procedure_en, (04.06.2017).

European Commission (2017e): Reflection Paper on the Deepening of the Economic and Monetary Union, Brussels: European Commission.

European Stability Mechanism (2017a): EFSF: An Active Issuer, https://www.esm.europa.eu/investors/efsf/efsf-active-issuer, (25.05.2017).

European Stability Mechanism (2017b): How we work, https://www.esm.europa.eu/about-us/how-we-work#overview, (25.05.2017).

European Stability Mechanism (2017c): History, https://www.esm.europa.eu/about-us/history, (25.05.2017).

European Systemic Risk Board (2015): ESRB report on the regulatory treatment of sovereign exposures, http://www.esrb.europa.eu/pub/pdf/other/esrbreportregulatorytreatmentsovereignexposures032015.en.pdf?c0cad80cf39a74e20d9d5947c7390df1, (24.05.2017).

European Union (2012): Treaty on the Functioning of the European Union

European Union (2013): COUNCIL REGULATION (EU) No 1024/2013 of 15 October 2013 conferring specific tasks on the European Central Bank concerning policies relating to the prudential supervision of credit institutions, http://eur-lex.europa.eu/legal-content/EN/TXT/PDF/?uri=CELEX:32013R1024&from=EN, (31.05.2017).

European Union (2014): REGULATION (EU) No 806/2014 OF THE EUROPEAN PARLIAMENT AND OF THE COUNCIL of 15 July 2014 establishing uniform rules and a uniform procedure for the resolution of credit institutions and certain investment firms in the framework of a Single Resolution Mechanism and a Single Resolution Fund and amending Regulation (EU) No 1093/2010, http://eur-lex.europa.eu/legal-content/EN/TXT/PDF/?uri=CELEX:32014R0806&from=EN, (31.05.2017).

FAZ (2015): Seehofer bezeichnet Griechenlands Handeln als «Zirkus», http://www.faz.net/agenturmeldungen/dpa/seehofer-bezeichnet-griechenlands-handeln-als-zirkus-13671501.html, (08.06.2017).

Feld, Lars P. / Osterloh, Steffen (2013): Is a fiscal capacity really necessary to complete EMU?, https://www.sachverstaendigenrat-wirtschaft.de/fileadmin/dateiablage/Sonstiges/Genshagen_Paper_-_Feld.pdf, (12.06.2017).

Feld, Lars P. / Schmidt, Christoph M. / Schnabel, Isabel / Wieland, Volker (2015): Divergence of liability and control as the source of over-indebtedness and moral hazard in the European Monetary Union, in: Baldwin, Giavazzi (Eds.): The Eurozone Crisis. A Consensus View of the Causes and a Few Possible Solutions, London: CEPR Presse, p. 185-197.

Feld, Lars P. / Schmidt, Christoph M. / Schnabel, Isabel / Wieland, Volker (2016): Causes of the Eurozone Crisis: A nuanced view, http://voxeu.org/article/causes-eurozone-crisis-nuanced-view, (20.05.2017)

Felipe, Jesus / Kumar, Utsav (2011): Unit Labour Costs in the Eurozone: The Competitiveness Debate Again, Annandale-on-Hudson: Levy Economics Institute Working Paper Collection.

Frankel, Jeffrey / Schreger, Jesse (2013): Over-optimistic official forecasts and fiscal rules in the eurozone, in: Review of World Economics, 149, p. 247-272.

Frankel, Jeffrey (2015a): The Euro Crisis: Where to from here?, in: Journal of Policy Modeling, 37, p. 428-444.

Frankel, Jeffrey (2015b): Causes of the Eurozone crises, in: Baldwin, Richard / Giavazzi, Francesco (Eds.): The Eurozone Crisis: A Consensus View of the Causes and a Few Possible Remedies, London: Centre for Economic Policy Research.

Fuest, Clemens / Becker, Johannes (2017): Der Odysseus Komplex. Ein pragmatischer Vorschlag zur Lösung der Eurokrise, München: Hanser Verlag.

Fuest, Clemens / Heinemann, Friedrich (2015): Accountability Bonds: Das Ausmaß der gemeinsamen Haftung eindämmen, http://www.euractiv.de/section/finanzen-und-wirtschaft/opinion/accountability-bonds-das-ausmass-der-gemeinsamen-haftung-eindammen/, (16.06.2017).

Gabrisch, Hubert / Staehr, Karten (2014): The Euro Plus Pact. Cost Competitiveness and External Capital Flows in the EU Countries, Working Paper Series, 1650, Frankfurt: European Central Bank.

Gerken, Lüder / Kullas, Matthias / Brombach, Till (2016): cepDefault-Index 2016. Creditworthiness trends of eurozone countries and other countries, Freiburg: Centre for European Policy.

Gerken, Lüder / Kullas, Matthias / Brombach, Till (2017): cepDefault-Index 2017. Creditworthiness trends of eurozone countries, Freiburg: Centre for European Policy.

German Council of Economic Experts (2011): Verantwortung für Europa wahrnehmen. Jahresgutachten 2011/12, Paderborn: Bonifatius GmbH Buch-Druck-Verlag.

German Council of Economic Experts (2012): The European Redemption Pact: An Illustrative Guide, https://www.sachverstaendigenrat-wirtschaft.de/fileadmin/dateiablage/download/publikationen/working_paper_02_2012.pdf, (12.06.2017).

German Council of Economic Experts (2013): Gegen eine rückwärtsgewandte Wirtschaftspolitik. Jahresgutachten 2013/14, Paderborn: Bonifatius GmbH Buch-Druck-Verlag.

German Council of Economic Experts (2014): Mehr Vertrauen in Marktprozesse, Jahresgutachten 2014/15, Paderborn: Bonifatius GmbH Buch-Druck-Verlag.

German Council of Economic Experts (2015): Consequences of the Greek Crisis for a More Stable Euro Area, Special Report (7), Wiesbaden: German Council of Economic Experts.

German Council of Economic Experts (2016): Zeit für Reformen. Jahresgutachten 16/17, Paderborn: Bonifatius GmbH Buch-Druck-Verlag.

Gros, Daniel / Mayer, Thomas (2010): How to deal with sovereign default in Europe: Towards a Euro(pean) Monetary Fund, http://voxeu.org/article/towards-european-monetary-fund, (22.05.2017).

Gros, Daniel / Mayer, Thomas (2011): Refinancing the EFSF via the ECB, Brussels: Centre for European Policy Studies.

Gros, Daniel (2013): Principles of a Two-Tier European Deposit (Re-)Insurance System, Brussels: CEPS.

Herwartz, Christoph (2015): Warum Merkel alles für Griechenland tun wird, http://www.n-tv.de/politik/politik_kommentare/Warum-Merkel-alles-fuer-Griechenland-tun-wird-article14763386.html, (16.06.2017).

Holzhausen, Arne / Sikova, Sabina (2015): Niedrigzinsen, Einkommen und Vermögen: Wer gewinnt, wer verliert, München: Economic Research Allianz.

Illing, Falk (2017): Die Eurokrise. Analyse der europäischen Strukturkrise, Wiesbaden: Springer.

Illing, Gerhard / König, Philipp (2014): Die Europäische Zentralbank als Lender of Last Resort, in: DIW (Eds.): DIW Wochenbericht, Berlin: DIW, p. 541-554).

International Monetary Fund (2013a): Greece. Ex Post Evaluation of Exceptional Access Under The 2010 Stand-By Arrangement, Washington: International Monetary Fund.

International Monetary Fund (2013b): Transcript of a Conference Call on Greece Article IV Consultation, http://www.imf.org/cn/news/articles/2015/09/28/04/54/tr060513, (03.06.2017).

International Monetary Fund (2016): Euro Area Policies, https://www.imf.org/external/pubs/ft/scr/2016/cr16219.pdf, (07.06.2017).

Ishiyama, Yoshihide (1975): The Theory of Optimum Currency Areas: A Survey, in: Staff Papers (International Monetary Fund), 22 (2), p. 344-383.

Jones, Marc (2015): Factbox: What is ECB Emergency Liquidity Assistance (ELA)?, http://www.reuters.com/article/us-eurozone-greece-ela-factbox-idUSKBN0P21XH20150622, (30.05.2017).

Juncker, Jean-Claude / Tusk, Donald / Dijsselbloem, Jeroen / Draghi, Mario / Schulz, Martin (2015): Completing Europe's Economic and Monetary Union, https://ec.europa.eu/commission/sites/beta-political/files/5-presidents-report_en.pdf, (15.06.2017).

Kirchgaessner, Stephanie (2016): EU finance ministers get tough with Italian bank trying for third bailout, https://www.theguardian.com/business/2016/jul/15/eu-finance-ministers-get-tough-with-italian-bank-trying-for-third-bailout, (05.06.2017).

Knauß, Ferdinand (2017): Für Macron bezahlen? Mit Vergnügen!, http://www.wiwo.de/politik/europa/knauss-kontert-fuer-macron-bezahlen-mit-vergnuegen-/19796482-all.html, (13.06.2017).

Krugman, Paul (1994): Competitiveness: A Dangerous Obsession, in: Foreign Affairs, 73, p. 28–44.

Krugman, Paul (2012): Revenge of the Optimum Currency Area, in: NBER Macroeconomics Annual, 27, p. 439-448.

Krugman, Paul (2015): The case for cuts was a lie. Why does Britain still believe it? The austerity delusion, https://www.theguardian.com/business/ng-interactive/2015/apr/29/the-austerity-delusion, (21.06.2017).

Landeszentrale für politische Bildung Baden-Württemberg (2017a): Finanzkrise in Griechenland, https://www.lpb-bw.de/finanzkrise_griechenland.html, (01.06.2017).

Landeszentrale für politische Bildung Baden-Württemberg (2017b): Euro-Krise, https://www.lpb-bw.de/euro_krise.html, (25.05.2017).

Lopez-Garcia, Paloma / di Mauro, Filippo / Altomonte, Carlo (2014): Micro-Based Evidence of EU Competitiveness. The Compnet Database, Frankfurt: ECB Working Paper Series.

Lopez-Garcia, Paloma / di Mauro, Filippo (2015): Assessing European competitiveness: the new CompNet micro-based database, Frankfurt: ECB Working Paper Series.

Maes, Ivo (1992): Optimum Currency Area Theory and European Monetary Integration, in: Tijdschrift voor Economie en Management, 37 (2), p. 137-152.

Mayer, Thomas (2013): Europas unvollendete Währung: Wie geht es weiter mit dem Euro?, Weinheim: Wiley-VCH Verlag.

McKinnon, Ronald I. (2015): Mundell, the Euro, and the World Dollar Standard, in: Journal of Policy Modeling, (37), p. 450-459.

Mersch, Yves (2016): Low interest rate environment – an economic, legal and social analysis, https://www.ecb.europa.eu/press/key/date/2016/html/sp161027.en.html, (30.05.2017).

Mersch, Yves (2017): Behaving responsibly in a low interest rate environment: A central banker's perspective, https://www.ecb.europa.eu/press/key/date/2017/html/sp170210.en.html, (30.05.2017).

Mitsopoulos, Michael / Pelagidis, Theordore (2011): The Real Cause of Greek Debt. Taxation and Labour Market Distortions in Greece, in: Intereconomics, 46 (2), p. 112-120.

Müller, Werner (2016): Staaten pfeifen auf Brüsseler Empfehlungen, http://www.faz.net/aktuell/wirtschaft/wirtschaftspolitik/die-eu-staaten-pfeifen-auf-das-bruesseler-fruehwarnsystem-12996062.html, (05.06.2017).

Müller, Peter / Neukirch, Ralf / Pfister, René / Sauga, Michael / Schult, Christoph (2017): Eine französische Affäre, in: Der Spiegel, 20, p. 17-20.

Mundell, Robert A. (1961): A Theory of Optimum Currency Areas, in: The American Economic Review, 51 (4), p. 657-665.

Mundell, Robert A. (1973): Uncommon arguments for common currencies, in: Johnson, Harry G. / Swoboda, Alexander K. (Eds.): The Economics of Common Currencies, London: Allen and Unwin.

Mussler, Werner (2016): Brüsseler Schlupflöcher für Bankenrettung, http://www.faz.net/aktuell/wirtschaft/eurokrise/italien/eu-wird-italien-die-rettung-von-monte-dei-paschi-wohl-nicht-verwehren-14589672.html, (05.06.2017).

Ongena, Steven / Popov, Alexander / Van Horen, Neeltje (2016): The invisible hand of the government: Moral suasion during the European sovereign debt crisis, Amsterdam: De Nederlandsche Bank Research Paper Series.

Pennekamp, Johannes / Schäfer, Manfred (2013): Weidmann kritisiert laxen Umgang mit Frankreich, http://www.faz.net/aktuell/wirtschaft/eurokrise/weidmann-umgang-mit-frz-defizit-problematisch-13479653.html, (21.06.2017).

Piller, Tobias (2014): Italiens Verrat, http://www.faz.net/aktuell/wirtschaft/kommentar-italiens-verrat-13012701.html, (23.05.2017).

Plickert, Philip (2017): Wovor die Euro-Kritiker schon früh warnten, http://www.faz.net/aktuell/wirtschaft/wirtschaftspolitik/25-jahre-maastricht-wovor-die-euro-kritiker-schon-frueh-warnten-14852243.html (18.05.2017).

Porter, Michael E. (1991): National Wettbewerbsvorteile: erfolgreich konkurrieren auf dem Weltmarkt, München: Droemer Knaur.

Robb, Greg (2015): Greek euro exit would be 'Lehman Brothers squared': economist, http://www.marketwatch.com/story/greek-euro-exit-would-be-lehman-brothers-squared-economist-2015-01-03, (16.06.2017).

Riehle, Gerhard (2016): Verzicht auf den Euro als Chance für Europa, Baden-Baden: Nomos.

Sala-i-Martin, Xavier / Schwab, Klaus (2014): The Global Competitiveness Report 2014–2015, Geneva: World Economic Forum.

Scharpf, Fritz W. (2011): Die Eurokrise: Ursachen und Folgerungen, in: Zeitschrift für Staats- und Europawissenschaften, 9 (3), p. 324-337.

Schieritz, Mark (2017): Zuchtmeister oder Zahlmeister?, http://www.zeit.de/2017/23/europaeische-union-euro-finanzminister-emmanuel-macron-angela-merkel, (10.06.2017).

Schui, Florian (2015): Wolfgang Schäuble learns from the wrong history book, http://www.voxeurop.eu/en/content/blog/4965075-wolfgang-schaeuble-learns-wrong-history-book, (16.06.2017).

Schult, Christoph (2017): Fast Hälfte der Deutschen will europäischen Finanzminister, http://www.spiegel.de/politik/ausland/frankreich-und-deutschland-sigmar-gabriel-fordert-elysee-2-0-a-1147428.html, (13.06.2017).

Sinn, Hans W. (2014): Chapter 9: Rethinking the euro system, in Sinn (Ed.): Euro Trap, Oxford: Oxford University Press.

Stiglitz, Joseph E. (2017): The Fundamental Flaws in the Euro Zone Framework, in: Nazaré, Costa C. / Gonçalves, José R. / Cunha Rodrigues, Nuno (Eds.): The Euro and the Crisis. Perspectives for the Eurozone as a Monetary and Budgetary Union, Cham: Springer International Publishing.

Tavlas, George S. (2009): Optimum-Currency-Area Paradoxes, in: Review of International Economics, 17(3), 536-551.

The Economist (2014): Ordoliberalism revisited. Two new books show that the euro crisis is far from over, http://www.economist.com/news/books-and-arts/21625654-two-new-books-show-euro-crisis-far-over-ordoliberalism-revisited, (16.06.2017).

Tower, Edward / Willett, Thomas (1976): The Theory of Optimum Currency Areas and Exchange Rate Flexibility: A More General Framework, Princeton: Princeton University Press.

Torres, Francisco (2008): The Role of Preferences and the Sustainability of EMU, in: Talani, Leila Simona (Ed.): The Future of EMU, Basingstoke: Palgrave Macmillan UK.

Trichet, Jean-Claude (2010): Interview with Jean-Claude Trichet, President of the ECB, and La Repubblica, conducted by Elena Polidori on Wednesday 16 June 2010, http://www.ecb.europa.eu/press/key/date/2010/html/sp100624.en.html, (01.06.2017).

Verdun, Amy (1999): The Role of the Delors Committee in the Creation of EMU: An Epistemic Community?, in: JEPP, 2, p. 308-328.

Watzlawek, Georg (2012): Merkel zieht mit klarer Kampfansage in den EU-Gipfel, http://www.handelsblatt.com/politik/deutschland/euro-bonds-nicht-solange-ich-lebe-merkel-zieht-mit-klarer-kampfansage-in-den-eu-gipfel/6804370.html, (13.06.2017).

Welt (2016): Varoufakis nennt Schäuble "inkompetenten kleinen Mann", https://www.welt.de/wirtschaft/article155359054/Varoufakis-nennt-Schaeuble-inkompetenten-kleinen-Mann.html, (08.06.2017).

Welter, Patrick (2013): Euro-Befürworter Mundell warnt vor Fiskalunion, http://www.faz.net/aktuell/wirtschaft/wirtschaftspolitik/oekonomen-konferenz-euro-befuerworter-mundell-warnt-vor-fiskalunion-12017336.html, (12.06.2017).

Winkler, Heinrich A. (2016): Geschichte des Westens: Die Zeit der Gegenwart, München: C. H. Beck.

Zenios, Stavros A. (2016): Fairness and reflexivity in the Cyprus bail-in, in: Empirica, 43, p. 579-606.

Zoli, Edda (2013): Italian Sovereign Spreads: Their Determinants and Pass-through to Bank Funding Costs and Lending Conditions, IMF Working Paper, 13/84, Washington: International Monetary Fund.

Zschäpitz (2016): Merkel kann Italiens Provokationen nicht kontern, https://www.welt.de/wirtschaft/article158298696/Merkel-kann-Italiens-Provokationen-nicht-kontern.html, (08.06.2017).

Zydra, Markus (2016): "Wir machen keinen Blindflug", http://www.sueddeutsche.de/wirtschaft/jens-weidmann-wir-machen-keinen-blindflug-1.3167249?reduced=true, (15.06.2017).